WINDSOR MOUNTAIN SCHOOL

WINDSOR MOUNTAIN SCHOOL

A Beloved Berkshire Institution

ROSELLE KLINE CHARTOCK

Foreword by Governor Deval Patrick

THE
History
PRESS

Published by The History Press
Charleston, SC 29403
www.historypress.net

Back cover, inset: Windsor Mountain School. *Courtesy of J.F. Samuels.*
Back cover, bottom: An aerial view of Windsor Mountain School taken from a school yearbook.

First published 2014

ISBN 978-1-5402-0999-3

Library of Congress CIP data applied for.

For Franny Hall (1918–2014), beloved Windsor Mountain teacher; for Windsor Mountain alumni; and for my beautiful family.

English and drama teacher Franny Hall at the blackboard. *From 1968 Windsor yearbook.*

Contents

CONTENTS

Foreword

I never visited Windsor Mountain School. Located in the town of Lenox, in the pastoral western Massachusetts area known as the Berkshires from 1944 to 1975, Windsor was about as far from me as a place could get. I grew up in poverty on the South Side of Chicago in the '50s and '60s, knowing nothing about such things as private boarding schools. By the time I got to Massachusetts, Windsor was in its waning days. By the time I discovered the Berkshires, Windsor was gone.

But we are connected.

Windsor was, in its day, one of more than three dozen private preparatory boarding schools in Massachusetts. Most were ancient havens of establishment for white Anglo-Saxon Protestants, exclusive and steeped in tradition and privilege. Windsor Mountain was unique. Unlike any of the others, Windsor was founded by German Jews, the Bondys, pioneers in humanistic education in their native land who were forced by the Nazis to give up their progressive boarding school in Germany. They founded Windsor on the premise that a diverse faculty and student body is the best way to help students from many backgrounds gain access to an excellent education and to teach about diversity. They were ahead of their time.

They were also right. And here's where Windsor and I connect.

In 1963, believing in the educational power of diversity, Heinz Bondy, Windsor Mountain's headmaster for twenty-five years, helped start A Better Chance (ABC), then a Boston-based program to identify high-achieving minority students for admission to private prep schools. The program has touched the lives of thousands of students of color and strengthened the educational experience at scores of private and even some public schools, and it continues to this day. In this book, Roselle Chartock recounts the arrival of the first ABC students at Windsor Mountain. It's a familiar scene. I was an ABC student at Milton Academy in Milton, Massachusetts, from 1970 to 1974. That opportunity changed my life's trajectory, as it has many others'. That was all the hook I needed when asked to write a foreword to a book about the life's work of one of ABC's founders.

Windsor made people better. My friends Jean and Peter Whitehead are uncommonly kind, engaging and thoughtful. They trace much of that to their experience at Windsor, which they both attended and where they met decades ago. Jeannie says that it was at Windsor Mountain that she was first inspired with the kind of "curiosity about the world that keeps you learning on your own." Peter is one of those old souls you meet who is singularly determined to do everything in his life with integrity. Their passion for the school is still palpable today.

I did eventually discover the Berkshires. We call this community home now, and the Whiteheads and Roselle and her husband, Alan, have become friends. The Bondys' humanistic philosophy is alive here. They taught, in words and deeds, the importance of honoring every student's individuality within a caring and democratic community. Windsor Mountain holds important lessons for schools today—and for whole communities, for that matter. We are all hungry to affirm such lessons. That's why this book is important. I hope the general reader will be inspired by this family's courage, wisdom and foresight, as well as by the beautiful and unique setting of the Berkshires, which was home to Windsor Mountain School.

DEVAL PATRICK
Governor, Commonwealth of Massachusetts
Richmond, Massachusetts
May 2014

Preface

Windsor Mountain School was created out of the desire by Drs. Max and Gertrud Bondy to make the world a better place. Having experienced the trauma of World War I and later persecution at the hands of the Nazis, the Bondys believed that through education, they could teach students respect for themselves and, in so doing, respect for others. Because of their Jewish heritage and uniquely democratic philosophy, the Bondys had been forced by the Nazis to sell their first school, Schule (School) Marienau, in 1936. And while this turn of events led to complicated feelings about their Jewish identity, it resulted in a humanistic philosophy endowed with lessons for educators and others concerned about education today. This book is about the Bondys, their philosophy and their school, Windsor Mountain.

An American version of Schule Marienau, Windsor Mountain School first opened in Windsor, Vermont, in 1939 and, in 1944, relocated to Lenox, Massachusetts, where it remained until its closing in 1975. An innovative, albeit often controversial, educational experiment and ahead of its time in honoring the individuality of every student, Windsor Mountain was the first co-ed, integrated boarding school in Berkshire County.[1] "What stood out [about Windsor]," wrote Catya von Karolyi, '72, "was their inclusiveness and freedom with responsibility, Dewey's philosophy. They had intentional multicultural education before most people were even aware of those concepts. They taught peace and stewardship" and, in Gertrud Bondy's

Students in front of the main manse at Windsor Mountain, preparing for a field trip. *From undated school catalogue.*

words, "not only academics, but the art of living, too." Recruiting students and faculty from all over the world, the Bondys encouraged their students to "be themselves" and to care about the welfare of others. Humanistic values, along with a strong and creative academic program, attracted well-known families like the Belafontes, Poitiers, Monks and Campanellas, who, upon arriving at the school, also fell in love with the Berkshires, an area that, ever since the nineteenth century, had been the summer home of wealthy families like the Vanderbilts, Choates and Carnegies and had lured writers like Melville, Hawthorne, Longfellow and Wharton. Later, it would lure others of note, including Norman Rockwell, Arlo Guthrie, Yo Yo Ma and James Taylor.

The story of Windsor Mountain School also reflects the social, political and economic changes of the twentieth century—"a political and social history wrapped around a school" is how Bill Dobbs, '69, put it—and prominently features events and names from local history, American history and pop culture.

Why Windsor Still Matters

Although there were some rough patches along the way that led to the school's closing in 1975, this book makes an argument for the kind of diversity and humanistic education that Windsor represented, especially important today, when America's schools are often seen as failing and when many states, in response, have turned to standardized testing as the answer to these problems, thus sacrificing students' individual needs and the creative energies of their teachers. Parents across the country have started to voice their opposition to such testing and are standing up for schools that address the emotional and psychological, as well as the intellectual, lives of their children.[2] Windsor Mountain represents a model for schools seeking ways to improve education without an inordinate amount of testing—the validity of which could surely benefit from closer scrutiny.

How This Book Came to be Written: Professional Connections to the Topic of Windsor Mountain

In 2009, in need of a compelling topic on which to do research during my sabbatical, I recalled that, decades earlier, back in 1972, a shy, blonde-haired boy from Windsor Mountain transferred into my history class at Monument Mountain Regional High School. I hadn't yet heard of Windsor, so I asked a colleague about it, and he said, "Oh, it's that hippie school up the road."

I went online for more information about Windsor Mountain and discovered that this topic combined three major areas of my professional research during forty-five years of teaching: education, local history and the Nazi Holocaust. This led to such questions as: How could the Bondys' progressive philosophy contribute to my role as an education professor?

What effect did the location of the school in the Berkshires have on students? (I lived and taught in the Berkshires and had designed a course on Berkshire history.) And, finally, what influence did the Bondys' Jewish heritage and their persecution by the Nazis have on their philosophy and school? (My colleagues and I created the first course on that subject for secondary students, and it was the focus of my first book.)

With these meaningful professional connections to Windsor Mountain, I knew I had found my research topic. More questions followed once I began interviewing Windsor alumni. For example, what was it about this school that had caused such an emotional connection among them? And could the topic of Windsor Mountain School and the Bondy family's personal saga turn into a compelling human-interest story? In my role as an academic, and not a graduate of the school, I set out to objectively tell Windsor's multi-layered story, and in the end, I came to believe that it was both an important story about education for these times and an important piece of Berkshire history.

PERSONAL CONNECTIONS TO THE BERKSHIRES

I love the Berkshires. As a child growing up in Hudson, New York, only an hour's drive from Lenox, I traveled with my family nearly every summer weekend to sit on the lawn and listen to concerts at Tanglewood, attend plays at the Berkshire Playhouse in Stockbridge and watch dancers at Jacob's Pillow in Becket—all idyllic excursions. I can recall the smell of spruce as we drove up the hill past Monument Mountain toward Stockbridge. Later, as a college student in the '60s, I waitressed at the Curtis Hotel and would hang out in the listening room at the Lenox Library during off hours, something many Windsor alumni told me they used to do. With these personal connections to the Berkshires, as well as those of my husband, it isn't hard to understand why we moved to the area in 1971.

This story, however, belongs to Windsor Mountain alumni, and, as much as possible, I have let them tell it.

CELEBRATING WINDSOR MOUNTAIN

The year 2014 marks Windsor Mountain School's seventy-fifth anniversary in America (and its seventieth anniversary in Lenox), its doors having first opened up in Windsor, Vermont, in 1939. So, *Windsor Mountain School: A Beloved Berkshire Institution* is a celebration of that anniversary and of the Bondys' legacy of humanistic education. And it is my sincere hope that the values that comprise that philosophy find their way into schools across the country, because every student deserves to be "recognized for who they are."

Berkshire scene on the Windsor campus. *From 1970 Windsor yearbook.*

Max [Bondy] *has built new ways for education, getting away from the tradition of educating through fear and drill.* [His] *teaching is about finding a new freedom which is not wild, but well-formed like beauty engraved in stone.*
—Gertrud Bondy, 1955 Windsor Mountain graduation

Acknowledgements

I want to sincerely thank everyone who contributed to this book, especially Bondy/Roeper family members and Windsor Mountain alumni and faculty. I enjoyed meeting and/or exchanging messages with dozens of people who gave generously of their time and memories. A list of their names follows the bibliography.

Certain people from that list deserve special mention, including, from the administration and faculty, the late Heinz Bondy and his wife, Carolyn Louks Bondy, as well as Maurice Eldridge, Frances "Franny" Benn Hall, Bob Blafield and Zuzana Wiener; members of the Bondy/Roeper family, including the late Annemarie Bondy Roeper and sons Peter and Tom Roeper, who shared materials from the Roeper family's archives; and Roeper School historian Marcia Ruff, whose knowledge and support were invaluable. Also deserving special mention is Karen Mireau, who collaborated with Annemarie on her memoir about Schule Marienau, and alumni Mark Abramowicz, Adrienne Belafonte Biesemeyer, Dave Bellar, Bill Dobbs, Pamela Esler, T.R. Jackson, Daniel Kegan, Judy Kirsch Levin, Bob Neaman (now deceased), Richard Neely, Stephan Ross and Jeannie Mercier Whitehead.

Thanks also go to Bob Gillette for introducing me to The History Press; to Vermont archivist Cathy Hoyt; to the *Berkshire Eagle* and the newspaper's librarian, Jeannie Maschino, and vice-president for news, Kevin Moran; to the librarians at both the Berkshire Atheneum (Local History section) in Pittsfield and the Lenox Library; to Chuck Hamilton for translating documents from German to English; and to John Andan for the Ghanaian connection.

Both Mike Cunningham and Beverly Greenfield provided information as well as access to the Boston University Tanglewood Institute's campus (formerly Windsor Mountain School). Barbara Dean was immensely helpful in transcribing recorded interviews, and a special thank-you goes to Nan Wile for her formatting skills, her calming and steady support and, most of all, her friendship. For scanning and preparing images for the book, thank you to Steve Carlotta of the Snap Shop in Great Barrington, who made it all look so easy.

Thanks also to the Massachusetts College of Liberal Arts for giving me the time to begin the research on this book and to President Mary Grant and the college's Education Department, who have always been extremely supportive.

And special thanks to Governor Deval Patrick for his contribution.

And to my editor, Tabitha Dulla, always responsive to my inquiries with a patient voice and wonderful guiding hand, thank you, and also to Will Collicott and Anna Burrous at The History Press.

Finally, words cannot express what I owe to my main reader and critic, best friend and love of my life, Alan, who knows a few things himself about telling stories. And to our children, Jonas and Sarah, and their families, who continue to integrate humanistic principles within their respective professions. Their love sustains me through every endeavor.

Chapter 1

The Bondy Family of Educators:
Six Life Stories

Bondy is a Jewish surname from the Sephardic personal name, Bondia, related to the Latin "bonus dies" or good day. It is used as a translation of Hebrew "Yom tov"…literally…"good day." The surname was borne by a family of Sephardic origin that settled in Prague, hence the occurrence chiefly in Bohemia and neighboring countries.[3]

Bondy/Bondia: a fitting name for a family of educators whose schools—spanning the entire twentieth century—were inspired by a desire to make the world a better place. Gerry Hausman, an English teacher at Windsor Mountain School from 1969 to 1975, put it succinctly when he said, "They were a dynamic family whose guiding principle was 'love conquers all.'"

What follows are the life stories of six members of the Bondy family and their connections to Windsor Mountain School and its humanistic philosophy. These stories describe extraordinary people, people not necessarily without flaws but remarkably courageous and creative in the ways that they—in the midst of more traditional institutions and times—provided a liberating environment in which students could freely explore their world and, in so doing, find themselves. Windsor students, faculty and others help to tell these stories.

MAX BONDY (1892–1951)

"Now, who was Max Bondy? First of all he was a German," wrote Ernst Cramer (1913–2010), a friend of the Bondy family.[4] A democratic humanist and dreamer, Max defined his New Humanism in one of his Sunday "Morning Talks" with students that were published in a booklet in 1936 at his first school, Schule Marienau, near Hamburg: "Only when the 'we' becomes an important, living and deciding factor in the life of an individual, can the 'I' be given human shape…The goal [of New Humanism] is reached when service for the community is accepted as destiny." But, he added, "To have [this] sense of community does not mean to give up totally one's own person." This balancing of the individual's needs with the well-being of the community would become the foundation of the Windsor Mountain School philosophy and the basis of Max and Gertrud's dream for making a better world.

Though he was a serious and sensitive man, Max had a lighter, more spontaneous side that those close to him knew well. One such person was Frances Benn Hall, affectionately known as Franny, scholar, playwright and poet, who with her husband, Jim, taught literature and theater at Windsor for most of the school's life. Said Hall:

> *Max might get up on a beautiful snowy morning and announce at breakfast, "It is a beautiful day. We cannot have school today. We are all going to Brodie* [Mountain in Pittsfield, Massachusetts]. *Get your skis; we will have Tuesday on Saturday." And we would. He was not as gentle as Gertrud; he could get very angry, but he was whimsical and friendly with the kids. If they needed him to teach history, "Alright I can do that sort of thing," he'd say, though he mostly acted as an administrator.*

Max's daughter, Annemarie Bondy Roeper, described her father as tall and slim, well built, but vain about his hair. "Later in his life, he would comb long strands of it over the bald spot on his head," she said. "He had a sense of humor about it. He had a name for each strand."[5] He was, she said, a very handsome man with a kind of aristocratic face. "He was proud of not looking Jewish, and he didn't have any of the features normally associated with being a Jew. He was fiercely committed to his German identity, rather than German Jewish culture. Women were just crazy about him, and he was crazy about women—just as my mother was crazy about men. There was

Max and Gertrud Bondy in the garden at Windsor Mountain School. *Courtesy of the Roeper family.*

a totally different attitude about relationships then, and theirs was what we might consider today a rather unorthodox marriage"[6] (what might be called an open marriage today).

Stefan Ross (Szmulek Rozental), '53, one of several teenage Holocaust survivors whom the Bondys took into the school in the late 1940s and early '50s, said that Max had a stern look but was a very warm, practical and sensitive man and that "when Humpty Dumpty would fall down, he could put Humpty Dumpties together again."

Max Bondy was born on May 11, 1892, in Hamburg-Blankenese and grew up in an assimilated German-Jewish family, upper class and liberal. His father, Solomon, the son of Leopold and Anna Bondy, owners of a bakery in the German town of Bohemia, made his way to Hamburg, Germany, at the age of fourteen, eventually becoming a multimillionaire in banking, real estate and importing sugar from Brazil.[7] On his way to adopting a strong German (as opposed to Jewish) identity, Max's father changed his name from Zigsmond (Solomon) to Siegfried and showed no outward signs of his past because, as his granddaughter Annemarie said, "it was better for business."

Anti-Semitism had grown in Germany in part out of the stereotype that all Jews were rich and owned all of the big businesses. Said Annemarie in her memoir, "My father, like his grandfather, never wanted to be identified as a Jew. And it was common at that time for many German Jews to think of themselves as Germans, not Jews."[8]

Siegfried Bondy and Max's mother, Mary Lauer, had five children. The only girl, Cornelia, or "Nelly" (1893), married a jurist, Manfred Zadik, and lived in England for many years. Curt Bondy (1894), referred to later as "Bo," was a professor of psychology and famous in his own right. Curt's twin brother, Walter, was killed "in friendly fire" in Romania in World War I,[9] and the youngest, Herbert "Fritz" (1902), a research chemist, left Germany for Holland in 1939 and lived in England until the end of his life.

In 1912–13, while studying art history at Frieburg University, Max began developing plans for a progressive school based on the ideals of the German Youth Movement. In an article titled "Die Grundlagen der Freischaridee" ("The Basics of a Fresh Idea"), Max outlined his humanistic educational philosophy.[10] Ida Gorres (1901–1971), a Czech Austrian writer, described the origins of the youth movement in her diaries, noting that it sprang up initially in Berlin when secondary school boys (much like Max and Curt), "bored to death by their homes and schools, and grownups in general, sought to elude this adult world by spending their Sundays and holidays roaming the countryside, hiking, an unheard of pursuit in those days. Hiking became symbolic, standing for Back to Nature against modern civilization."[11] "They were rather like hippies in the 1960s in the U.S. in that way," Annemarie said.[12]

In 1914, Max volunteered as an artillery officer in World War I, but when he was wounded in the war and home on furlough in 1916, he became active again, this time as a leader in the youth movement, which was composed of several branches. Some were Christian assimilationists and welcomed Jews; others banned them and were fiercely anti-Semitic. There were Protestant and Catholic branches, as well as all-Jewish groups, split into Zionists and anti-Zionists. And while the movement was supposedly nonpolitical, there were right-wing groups, extreme nationalists and those on the left who advocated democracy.

At a 1916 convention of the movement's leaders, held for the purpose of addressing the "Jewish Question," Max spoke up during the debate about whether certain branches should accept Jews. He said that most Jews did not fit into the youth movement. "There are certain *imponderables* [his italics]," he said, "that remain strange to the average Jew, who lack a certain freshness and simplicity...I would not be surprised if the majority of Jews asking to be admitted were rejected."[13] This attitude among Jews attending the convention, according to Walter Laqueur, "revealed what can only be described as a certain lack of dignity." He cites Max's quote—which Tom Roeper says portrays his grandfather in an "unflattering light"—and says that Bondy was among the Jewish members who justified the quota that allowed only a certain number of Jews to join a group. Max was apparently not willing to sacrifice his alliance with German culture for a faith he hadn't practiced in the first place. Perhaps his compromises were in response to such statements as this from one of the delegates: "A Jew is not suitable for us even if he is baptized ten times over."

Whatever Max's attitudes about his Jewish heritage, he nevertheless despised Nazism and viewed it as a huge departure from the German culture he loved. And when he was asked to leave the youth movement, he was devastated, as he was when the Nazis later forced him to give up his school.

Because of his personal encounter with Nazism and the unspeakable atrocities he observed from afar during the Second World War, Max's fierce nationalism eventually mellowed. In a talk he gave in 1947, at the end of a summer spent in Europe, Max tried to instill in the audience of German young people hope for the future and told them that they must "try to convince the world that political nationalism is at the end of its development [and] that humanity is ready for the idea of one world."

After World War I, Max earned his PhD in art history (1919) from the University of Erlangen. He had married his first cousin Gertrud Wiener three years earlier, on September 30, 1916 (her mother, Olga, and Max's mother, Mary, were sisters), and they had three children born three years apart: Annemarie (1918–2012); Ursula Babette, or "Ulla" (1921–1970); and Heinz Gustav Eric (1924–2014), all of whom were baptized as Lutherans upon Heinz's birth. Annemarie said in her memoir that Max converted because (1) he never wanted to be identified as a Jew and (2) he was "a very convinced Christian and believed strongly in Christian ideals" ("like forgiveness and acceptance," said his grandson Tom Roeper), while Gertrud thought conversion might save the family from discrimination.[14] Despite the emancipation of Jews throughout the German states in 1871—or perhaps because of it—anti-Semitism was still ever present, and respected philosophers at the time, like Hartwig von Hundt-Radowsky, "advised expulsion of the Jews…and hinted that their murder would be no more than a transgression."[15]

In 1920, four years after their marriage, Max and Gertrud opened their first school in Erlangen, then relocated to Gandersheim in 1923 and eventually, with financial help from his father, moved the school to a large estate in Marienau, near Hamburg, in 1928–29. There, they ran Schule Marienau, their private progressive boarding school, until 1936, when the Nazis—who, by then, were no longer allowing Jews to educate Aryan children—forced the Bondys to give up their school.[16] With passage of the Nuremberg Laws in 1935, Jews were stripped of their civil rights, citizenship and property, and Max, though a convert to Lutheranism, was, as far as the Nazis were concerned, still a Jew. Said Annemarie, "One day a world of their own, then nothing." Max became a "broken man" and, unlike her mother, never really adapted to the loss.[17] (Years later, a democratic German government also recognized the Bondys' Jewish heritage, albeit with more humane purposes: members of the family received reparations periodically to make up for the property and professions taken from them during the Nazi years, according to Tom Roeper.)

No longer in possession of their beloved school, and in the midst of growing danger, the Bondys came to realize they would need to leave Germany, though Max was reluctant to do so. With the help of George Roeper, their son-in-law, and Harald Baruschke, their former student at Schule Marienau, the Bondys were able to secure passports that didn't identify them as Jews. Also helpful were the international contacts of educator Paul Geheeb, one of Max's closest confidents. (Geheeb's boarding school, Oldenwaldschule, and Schule Marienau were considered among the most daring and modern educational and international experiments of their time, according to Barbara Kersken, Schule Marienau's current historian.)

In 1936, Gertrud, Ulla and Heinz were the first of the family to immigrate to Switzerland, where Gertrud established Ecole de Les Rayons at a former Quaker school in Gland, near Lake Geneva. Harald Baruschke had opened the school earlier, and it soon became a haven for Jewish children escaping from Europe.

Max and Annemarie arrived in Switzerland in 1937, soon after Annemarie graduated from Schule Marienau, which was already in the hands of Dr. Bernard Knoop, an educator from a more conservative wing of the boarding school movement. Max had stayed in Germany longer, in part, because he believed Hitler would not last and that he would be able to retrieve his school.

As war was brewing, and afraid that they wouldn't be safe in Switzerland either, the family left after two years for the United States, where they arrived in April 1939, staying first in New York City. George Roeper had gone to Vermont earlier in November 1938 to secure property there, and in the summer of 1939, Max and Gertrud's first undertaking in their new country began when they ran a summer camp at Lake Winnipesaukee, New Hampshire,[18] followed by the opening that fall of their first school in the United States, the Windsor Mountain School, located briefly in Windsor, Vermont (1939–40), then Manchester (1940–44) and, finally, Lenox, Massachusetts (1944–75).

The Bondys, like several other noted educators and professionals emigrating from Germany and Austria, had been sponsored by three well-known intellectuals: prize-winning journalist Dorothy Thompson (1893–1961), the first American journalist to be expelled from Nazi Germany and one of the founders of the Emergency Rescue Committee; Thompson's friend the novelist and poet Thomas Mann, also a German émigré (1875–1955); and author, educator and activist Dorothy Canfield Fisher, who introduced Montessori education to the United States.[19] All three had assisted other refugees from Nazi Germany, among them Carl Zuckmayer (1896–1977), the noted playwright and screenwriter (*The Blue Angel*, 1930, starring Marlene Dietrich), who briefly settled in Vermont and sent his daughter, Winnetou, to Windsor Mountain. The fact that Thompson; her husband, Sinclair Lewis; and Dorothy Canfield Fisher were residents of the Windsor area might have drawn these refugees to the area.

During the mid-'40s, Max pursued his dream of buying back Schule Marienau and running both schools after the war. But that was not to

Windsor Mountain logo indicating that the Bondys' first school began in 1920. *From undated Windsor brochure.*

be, in part, because of U.S. legislation forbidding American citizens from acquiring property in Germany at that time. So Windsor Mountain School became the Bondys' Schule Marienau in America, and they would date Windsor's founding not as 1939 but 1920, when their very first school opened in Germany. And it is the year 1920 that appears on Windsor's logo.

Although Max and Gertrud were forced to leave Schule Marienau behind, they nevertheless brought with them to America their humanistic philosophy of education and many of the beloved traditions they had developed there. One of those traditions was the celebration of Max's birthday. "No school that day," teacher Franny Hall said, "and I always had to do a full-length play in honor of Max that night." At six o'clock in the morning, the students, wearing white shirts and blue jeans, the school's colors, would go to the main house and stand under the window where Max and Gertrud were sleeping and sing together in Latin "Gaudeamus Igitur" ("So Let Us Rejoice"), a song in the tradition of "Carpe Diem," or "Seize the Day," with its exhortations to enjoy life. Later in the day, Max would give a birthday speech in which he would share again the meaning of the Bondys' philosophy. Gertrud continued that tradition after Max's death, which came just seven years after Windsor's move to Lenox.

Max Bondy died of leukemia in the Peter Bent Brigham Hospital in Boston on April 6, 1951, at the age of fifty-eight. A pioneer in the German Youth Movement, the Country Boarding School Movement and the progressive education movement both in Germany and America, Max survived the atrocities of World War I and persecution at the hands of the Nazis. The school that he and Gertrud had founded, Schule Marienau, continues to this day and is one of the leading boarding schools in Germany. His obituary in the April 16, 1951 *Berkshire Eagle*, "Dr. Bondy Dies at 58 in Boston," noted that his "funeral was held in Lenox at the Trinity Episcopal Church with Reverend Robert S.S. Whitman, Rector officiating." Besides Gertrud and their son, Heinz (who became headmaster for the next twenty-five years), Max was "survived by Mrs. George Roeper [Annemarie] of Detroit, Michigan, and Mrs. Donald Gerard [Ursula] of Worcester and five grandchildren."[20] Max is buried in Mountainview Cemetery on Housatonic Street in Lenox, Massachusetts.

Gertrud Wiener Bondy (1889–1977)

"Thank You for Letting Me Be Myself, Again," the song by Sly and the Family Stone (1969), could serve as the mantra of hundreds of Windsor Mountain students who testified that Gertrud Bondy saved their lives by letting them be who they are.

In her seven-page memoir, "My Personal History," written in 1970, the year of Windsor Mountain School's fiftieth anniversary, Gertrud, then eighty, wrote, "My study of psychoanalysis has helped me in my work. Without using therapy as it is generally understood, I [try] to give young people a feeling of security and of being accepted as a person."

In an excerpt from a recorded speech welcoming Windsor students back to spring semester in 1963, and speaking with a soft European accent in a voice endowed with natural authority, Gertrud echoed Max's message about a caring community in balance with every student's unique interests: "Spring is here…and there's an awakening all around us. I often say, 'wake up,' and I always mean to look around and see and to think. And if you think, you will see you are no longer the center of the world, and you learn to give to those who need it." Both Max and Gertrud believed that education had to build character *and* nurture critical thinking. And interestingly, both aims were manifested by Gertrud in a very physical way, according to Arthur Myers in an October 13, 1961 *Berkshire Eagle* article titled "Student of Sigmund Freud Reminisces": "[Gertrud Bondy] is a tall, handsome woman, with the sort of charm seldom seen in this country and probably rare now in Europe. She is aristocratic in bearing and intellectual in conversation, yet she radiates warmth and gentleness."

Windsor Mountain students derived comfort from sitting on Gertrud's bed and talking with her whenever they visited her apartment on the second floor of the main house. Gigi Buffington, '74, said, "It was therapy, but we didn't know it." "She would read Goethe to us," recalled Fred Burstein, '68. Roselle Van Nostrand, '74, often visited the sitting room outside Gertrud's bedroom where she held her "salon" and where everyone was welcome: "I spent almost every evening with Gertrud. It was my refuge. She always had on a hand-woven, lightweight shawl. [I remember] her white hair…It was like a tea party. There were always the demitasse gold-rimmed cups and Pepperidge Farm cookies…You could say what you wanted. You couldn't shock this lady."

Zuzana Wiener, who taught history and Russian language at Windsor and was the wife of Jan "Gerdi" Wiener, Gertrud's nephew, smiled as she

28

Gertrud Bondy. *Courtesy of the Roeper family.*

described Gertrud's "beautiful lace nightgowns and little brocade coat. She would talk about sex and drugs and everything. And [all the while] she would be puffing on a cigarette with one hand, and with her left hand, she could do a braid—three strands with only one hand!"

Steve Peskin, '54, who became a mathematics teacher in New York City and died of lung cancer in 2000, was particularly close to Gertrud, according to his wife, Martha, who said that Steve had gone to Windsor because he "had troubles as a teenager and Windsor gave him hope; it was a life-saver for him. Many kids there were troubled, from wealthy families and very bright; they'd talk to Gertrud and feel better." While Martha said that Gertrud didn't have favorites, she did say that Gertrud "took [Steve] under her wing," the implication being that she might have bonded with some students more than others. Some of the interviewees believed that Gertrud most assuredly favored a certain few but always responded to everyone's needs.

Gertrud Wiener Bondy was born on October 7, 1889, in Prague, then part of Austria. The daughter of Olga Lauer and Gustav Wiener, who managed several textile factories there, Gertrud's was a cultured, highly educated Jewish family, and her house in Prague was, like Max's in Hamburg, a center of contemporary cultural debate, according to Barbara Kersken.[21] The family eventually moved to Vienna, but after her father's death and her mother's second marriage, when Gertrud was seventeen, they moved to Hamburg.

While growing up in Prague, Gertrud attended a private girls' school and studied piano with the idea of becoming a concert pianist. She would play for her father, Gustav, who, she mentions in her *Personal History*, despite being blind was an avid mountain climber like everyone else in the family. Gertrud's two siblings included an older brother, Julius, or "Jula," and an older sister, Mathilde, or "Mathy" (sometimes spelled Matti).

Later in her life, Mathy came to live and teach at Windsor Mountain after her husband, Paul Lauer, died. She soon became known as the "disciplinarian," said Franny Hall, who recalled Mathy saying, "All the children must love Gertrud; there has to be a wicked witch, and I'll be the one who says, 'No, you can't go out after dark.'" Mathy died on May 29, 1958, at Windsor while working on a play with her German class. (Not only had *she* married a cousin, but so, too, did Gertrud, who was Max's first cousin. "It was common during those days," said Annemarie. "It was always on my mind, though, that the children of first cousins might turn out to be either idiots or geniuses. It haunted me all my life."[22])

Gertrud eventually decided to become a doctor instead of a concert pianist, and in 1914, she entered the university to study medicine. While doing her clinical work on the job in a children's hospital—her studies having been interrupted by World War I—she heard the lectures of Professor Sigmund Freud, and thus began her interest in analysis and psychiatry. In her *Personal History*, she wrote about becoming Freud's student and completing her own analysis in Vienna in 1921 with Freud's early colleague, Dr. Otto Rank. Annemarie said that "psychoanalysis was like a religion in [her mother's] circles."

After Gertrud married Max in 1916, she returned to Vienna to continue her studies, and by 1918, their eldest child, Annemarie, was born, followed by Ursula in 1921 and Heinz in 1924.

When Max and Gertrud opened their first school in 1920 in Erlangen, they began fulfilling the ideals of the German Youth Movement, which scorned the hypocrisy of the times and some of the more dubious traditions among students. In one of her morning speeches at Windsor Mountain School, Gertrud spoke graphically about one of the "uglier customs" of German fraternities, dueling, "in which they hit and cut each other's faces. It was actually considered a great honor to look like beefsteaks and to have a face that was cut through and through." Such customs were among the reasons Max and Gertrud believed that a "new method of educating young people was necessary."[23]

But their dream of helping young people develop tolerance and civility, their "new method of educating," was temporarily halted when they were forced to sell their school and flee Nazi Germany in 1936. Eventually, however, they continued that dream when they opened Windsor Mountain School in 1939 in Vermont.

During Windsor's thirty-one years in Lenox, Gertrud avoided any discussion of the family's Jewish heritage, the role it played in forcing them out of Germany or its role in the development of the school's philosophy. Members of her family and, later, several students were critical of this silence. Zuzana Wiener, wife of Gertrud's nephew Jan (pronounced Yon), said that Gertrud never admitted she was a Jew, which Zuzana thought was odd since many of Gertrud's relatives, including her brother Jula (Jan's father), died because of their religion. Peter Roeper, a grandson of Gertrud's, pointed out that "for people who scorned the hypocrisy [of their times]," his grandparents were, themselves, guilty of hypocrisy in keeping silent about their heritage. Peter wrote in an e-mail, "[T]he school that encouraged psychological awareness denied an elemental psychological factor: who and where the leaders of the school and the philosophy of the school came from, a hidden fact, perhaps even a shame." (Annemarie, Peter's mother and Gertrud's daughter, wrote in her memoir, "Even before the Nazis, there was conflict in our family regarding our Jewishness." And Peter Bondy, another grandson, said his father, Heinz, never discussed his Jewish heritage. "I didn't realize for awhile that my father had a Jewish background.")

Bill Dobbs, '69, a lawyer and gay activist, reported that no one at the school had any idea that the Bondys were Jewish and had even had to escape Nazi Germany. He said that he and other students only found out when Gerdi (Jan) Wiener told them the story in history class of his own escape from the Nazis. Dobbs said the students were stunned that day upon making this discovery. Zuzana Wiener described that episode and Gertrud's response to it:

> When Jan was teaching a history class and told the story about how his father died (he committed suicide rather than be taken by the Nazis) students asked him, "How come you are Jewish, Jan, and your aunt is not?" Then, after one of the students went to Gertrud and told her Jan's story, she called Jan to her room and said, "If you will teach here and you will be saying these things, you will have to leave." And Jan said, "Are you serious? Your brother died because he was Jewish, and you are telling me that I can't admit I'm a Jew? Well, I'm leaving." Gertrud called him later. I remember that phone call. Gertrud was crying and told Jan, "No, no, no, of course you will not leave."

Jenny Roper, niece of George Roeper and Annemarie, confirmed this story about Gertrud reprimanding Gerdi for mentioning the family's heritage. She observed, "The Bondys were very tolerant and pro-diversity but were less so when it came to their own people." A number of family members are still disturbed by Gertrud's silence, while others justify it. Ellen Winner, daughter of Tom Winner (Gertrud's nephew and Jan's brother), admitted that the Bondys were conflicted about their Judaism and never made their heritage clear. Her parents, Tom and Irene, "talked about that fact, and a lot of us in the family thought it wasn't good."

Tom Roeper, a grandson of Max and Gertrud's (whom, he said, they all called Mutti, or mother), tried to make sense of what role, if any, their Jewish heritage played in forming the Bondys' humanistic philosophy of education:

Max [and Mutti] *agreed to hide their Jewish origins and were criticized by many people for that, much as some people criticize light-skinned blacks for "passing"* [as white]. *Curt (Max's brother) criticized them for it. Max was largely indifferent to the Jewish religion and, if anything, really did reject it long before the Nazis came to power, as did his mother, apparently. Huge numbers of Jewish people did that in Germany. On the other hand—and this is important—much about the Bondys reflected Jewish culture, the devotion to talking, introspection and the legitimacy of Freudian approaches. That is the really significant historical connection, I think, if one wants to grasp from where their philosophy emerged.*

On the other hand, Kathleen "Kay" Gerard Whitney pointedly justified her grandparents' decision to remain silent, noting that it was their right to do so since they had never felt any alliance to that heritage. And Tom Roeper agreed that "Max Bondy and his father had every right to decline a particular religious label."[24]

Whenever the Bondys' heritage came up during my interviews with dozens of Windsor Mountain graduates, many of whom are themselves Jewish, their reactions ranged from mild surprise to shock and disappointment. Judith Kirsch Levin, '58, for example, said upon hearing this information for the first time, "The Bondys' message to us about tolerance and peace would have had more meaning for me if they had shared their personal experiences and background."

Even Hadassah "Dossy" Silberstein, '56, said, "It never occurred to me to think that the Bondys were Jewish," and this comment from the daughter of the principal of the Pittsfield Jewish Community Hebrew School, Jacob "Jake" H. Pecker, who helped prepare some of Windsor's Jewish students, like Charles Landau, for their Bar Mitzvah and whom the Bondys had asked to be available for Windsor's Holocaust orphans who often spent the Jewish holidays with Dossy's family.

Zuzana said that Gertrud's silence might have been masking her pain and her fear of anti-Semitism, the horrors of which she had experienced firsthand in Germany and—it should be noted—a prejudice that wasn't uncommon in the Berkshires in the 1940s, when the Bondys first arrived. Several schools had quotas then, and country clubs and other venues were closed to Jews. Even now, such prejudice still exists, according to an article in the April 1, 2014 *Boston Globe* titled "Anti-Semitic Incidents Rose in Mass in 2013."[25] So, said Bill Dobbs, "Gertrud's silence may have been a conscious self-preservation strategy," a way of protecting herself and her family.

While reasons for Gertrud's decision to keep silent about her heritage might not be fully known, what *is* clear is that many Windsor students believe that their talks with Gertrud saved their lives. Music teacher Bob Blafield, founder of the Berkshire Lyric Theater and Chorus, noted still another part of her humanistic philosophy that might have endeared students to Gertrud: "her liberal attitude towards sex." (Annemarie confirmed this in her 2012 memoir, in which she wrote, "They [my parents] believed in free love. Any honest relationship was acceptable."[26]) "One day," Blafield said, "I saw teenagers lounging around the swimming pool in what seemed to be white swimsuits. Looking more closely, I saw they were all naked." Gertrud's response: "This is not a problem." And with a smile, he remembered something she once said to him so many years ago: "You know, Bobby, someday everyone will be a nice cocoa color, and what's wrong with that?"

When Windsor closed in 1975, Gertrud went to live with her daughter, Annemarie, and son-in-law, George Roeper, who had, in 1941, created a successful private day school, The Roeper School, in Michigan. Steve Peskin visited her there, as he had always done each summer at Windsor Mountain, where he used to chauffeur her around in her silver Chevy Impala convertible (which was "a mile long") with the black top down. That was one of her favorite activities, "especially in winter wrapped in blankets," said Jenny Roper. Peskin would take Gertrud on the drives she had always loved, "but," said his wife, Martha, "he felt depressed because Gertrud was no longer surrounded by the physical and mental amenities she'd had at Windsor Mountain School."

The "soul of Windsor Mountain School," and one of the first female doctors and psychoanalysts in the world, Gertrud Bondy, died on April 30, 1977, at the age of eighty-eight and is buried with Max in Mountainview Cemetery. She was survived by Heinz and Annemarie and eight grandchildren, as well as hundreds of students who carry on her legacy—which brings to mind one more of Franny Hall's memories: "When [Jim and I] adopted Catie, we wanted Gertrud to be her godmother. And she said, 'At my age, Franny, I may not be a good choice.' And we said, 'We want her to have something of you in her.'" Catie is now a physician on an Indian reservation in Montana.

ANNEMARIE BONDY ROEPER (1918–2012)

The eldest daughter of Max and Gertrud Bondy, Annemarie was the recorder of her family's history and the founder, with her husband, George, of The Roeper School (1941) in Michigan, one of the longest continuously running schools for gifted learners in America.

At the November 2012 convention of the National Association for Gifted Children, five months after her death, there was a "Tribute to the Wisdom of Annemarie Roeper," at which people shared the story of how Annemarie and George founded The Roeper School, where students, by learning to think critically and to appreciate tolerance and democracy, would learn not to follow leadership blindly as they believed so many people had done between the wars. They put into practice the humanistic philosophy they had both benefitted from while students at her parents' school in Marienau, about which Annemarie wrote a memoir, *Marienau, A Daughter's Reflections*.

Annemarie Martha Bondy Roeper was born on August 27, 1918, in Vienna, one of three children born to Max and Gertrud. She was among the youngest students, and first females, at her parents' school, Schule Marienau, which she attended secretly at first until coeducation became a legal option. There, she met George Roeper (1910–1992), a respected student leader whose father had built a successful import-export firm, leading to his raising his family for many years in Kobe, Japan. George's parents sent him to Marienau in 1923, when he was thirteen and Annemarie only five years old. She recalled that by 1936, when she was eighteen, she and George became lovers but were not allowed to marry—despite the fact that she had been baptized a Lutheran—because the 1935 Nuremberg Laws prohibited Jews from marrying Christians. They finally married upon arriving in New York City in April 1939.

Even after the family was forced to give up Schule Marienau, Annemarie and Max stayed on at the school until she graduated in the spring of 1937; then they followed Gertrud to Switzerland.[27] And after learning from a former classmate at Marienau that his life was in danger for helping Jews, George, too, fled and joined the Bondys and their staff of thirteen teachers, including Annemarie, at Les Rayons, their new school in Switzerland.

Despite the potential dangers, Annemarie decided to return to Vienna in the fall of 1937 to study medicine, intending to become a psychoanalyst like her mother. Gertrud had arranged for her to meet Freud and his daughter, Anna, and in 1938, she visited with them at their house at Bergstrasse 19, "a

Annemarie and George Roeper. *Courtesy of the Roeper family*.

very comfortable house," wrote Annemarie, "[his] office as memorable as the conversation we had there." The next day, however, the Nazis picked up Anna Freud for interrogation, leading soon after to the Freuds' escape to England.[28] The dangers now very clear, Annemarie decided to leave and was able to catch the last train to cross the Austrian border before the Nazis annexed the country in the Anschluss of March 1938. She recalled that at the border with Prague, people who looked Jewish were being taken off the train by Nazis. "It was," she said, "a miracle I was saved because I didn't look Jewish," though the Nazis had put an end to her ever finishing medical school.

Prior to the Bondys' arrival in New York City, George had gone to Vermont—in the fall of 1938—to line up property for the family to start another school. That school, Windsor Mountain, opened in Windsor, Vermont, in the fall of 1939. George and Annemarie returned to Vermont in September 1940 to work briefly at the school, which by that time had already moved to Manchester.

In 1941, Annemarie and George decided to move to Detroit, where they had been invited by two Viennese psychoanalysts, Drs. Richard and Editha Sterba, friends of Max and Gertrud's, to direct the Edith Sterba Nursery School in Highland Park, Michigan, a psychoanalytically-oriented K–1 school for developmentally disabled children.[29] The Roepers added a grade school and moved the school to Detroit in 1942. Then in 1946, they purchased a campus in Bloomfield Hills, Michigan, where they renamed the school City and Country School of Bloomfield Hills, with ninety students through grade six. By 1956, the Roepers had embraced the mission of educating gifted and talented students, and in 1981, they expanded to include an upper school on a second campus in Birmingham, Michigan. Said Annemarie, "We would help them [the gifted] because we needed them to help the world."[30]

George retired in 1979, and a year later, at the age of sixty-two, Annemarie decided to leave. Together they moved to California and opened a consultation service in El Cerrito. They were living then in nearby Oakland, where, said Annemarie, they survived "a second holocaust," the firestorm of October 1991, which destroyed their home and all of their possessions. Fortunately, prior to the fire, the headmaster at Schule Marienau at the time, Wolf-Dieter Hasenclever, had sent two of his staff to Annemarie's house to bring some boxes containing Windsor and Roeper archives back to the school in Germany. Today, some of the surviving materials are located at The Roeper School. These archives now include a film about the Bondys and their schools, *Across Time and Space* (2002, Searchlight Films), made by Ashley James and his wife, Kathryn Golden, whose child was a client of Annemarie's in California. The DVD offers glimpses of the Roeper and Windsor Mountain Schools in America, as well as Schule Marienau, along with references to the Holocaust and the Bondys' escape from the Nazis.

In the film, Annemarie says that she wanted to document the history of the schools and to make clear the Bondys' Jewish heritage, though Jenny Roper said, "It was only after Annemarie retired that she began to talk about being Jewish." Wrote her son, Peter Roeper:

> *At this particular time* [2002], *the school was considering writing some kind of history of the school, and they did not involve her in this*

discussion. This made her furious. It was the [filmmakers] *who actually wanted to emphasize the Jewish history of the family, and it became a subject of considerable discussion within the family that had not occurred before. Even today, the subject of Jewishness is a difficult issue for the family to address.*

Heinz Bondy, Annemarie's brother, told me he wasn't pleased with the film because "there was not much at all in it about Windsor Mountain," where he was headmaster from 1951 to 1975.

When George died in 1992 at the age of eighty-two, The Roeper School website described his and Annemarie's fifty-two years together as "a marriage of equals" and George as "handsome and charismatic" and "a spokesman for the school and its humanistic philosophy." Like Max and Gertrud, he is buried in Mountainview Cemetery in Lenox, Massachusetts.

Annemarie died twenty years later, on May 11, 2012, in Oakland, California, at the age of ninety-three. The press release issued by the school noting her death contained many of her and George's contributions, in particular, their founding of The Roeper School, for which Eastern Michigan University awarded them honorary doctorates in 1978, a poignant gesture, considering that, because of the Nazis, both were unable to complete or receive the degrees on which they were working.

All three of the Roepers' offspring—Dr. Thomas Roeper (born 1943), Windsor graduate Peter Roeper (born 1946) and Karen Roeper (born 1949)—continue the Bondy/Roeper legacy in their respective roles as educators.

HEINZ GUSTAV ERIC BONDY (1924–2014)

Heinz Bondy, the youngest of Max and Gertrud's three children, was a strong advocate for students and a reluctant headmaster of Windsor Mountain School from 1951 to its closing in 1975. Heinz's motto, "Adjust, Don't Conform," was so meaningful to the organizers of Windsor's 1996 reunion that they had T-shirts made up with the slogan. It was also a headline in the February 15, 1963 *Berkshire Eagle*, "Toward Adjustment, Away from Conformity," part of a series of articles on the area's fifteen independent schools. But besides his motto, what most people remembered about Heinz was his passion for sports, soccer in particular.

Heinz Bondy at the edge of the baseball field. *From 1958 Windsor catalogue.*

Soccer had been good to Heinz Bondy. He had played in Switzerland at Les Rayons, the school his parents operated after fleeing Germany, and it had led to a scholarship to Swarthmore College in Pennsylvania, from which he graduated in 1949. Heinz's son, Peter, said his father loved talking sports and was "a soccer all-American who once trained for the U.S. Olympics team but broke his arm," apparently putting an end to that dream.

As soccer coach and history teacher at Windsor Mountain for fifteen of the twenty-five years he served as headmaster, Heinz watched as his teams got better and better, especially after he took the unusual step of recruiting students from abroad, specifically from Ghana and Kenya, places where soccer was far more popular a sport than it was in America at that time. One of those students was Cadman Mills, '63, who went on to get his PhD in economics at Boston College and to become senior economics advisor to his brother, John Atta Mills, the late president of Ghana. He currently serves as ambassador from Ghana to the United States. Said Mills, "Soccer was Heinz's passion, and he was happy when we [the African students] improved the school's reputation in soccer. When I was there, Windsor became the Western New England champions."

Even years after the African students graduated, Windsor continued to have winning teams. Once, when they were invited to play West Point, Terry Hall, '69, recalling that game, beamed and said, "We won!" In the end, Heinz Bondy took great pride in these accomplishments, and there was little question that he was happiest around a field, whether it was a soccer or baseball field.

Heinz Eric Bondy was born on June 2, 1924, in Gandersheim, Germany, where Max and Gertrud had established School Community Gandersheim (1923), which, five years later, moved to Marienau. Heinz described how he had attended the school at Marienau from its inception in 1928, when he was four, to shortly before the family had to leave Germany, in 1936. Peter Bondy, one of Heinz's two sons, said that he recalled hearing about their escape, when the family had to sneak across the Swiss border with Max driving the car "and Heinz and Mutti [Gertrud] in the trunk."

After the Bondys arrived in New York in April 1939, leaving behind their Swiss school, Les Rayons, Heinz said, "We all stayed in one hotel room." And with the help of the Lutheran church, "I initially went to a Lutheran private school in Connecticut." By the fall of that year, the family had settled in Vermont, with Max and Gertrud now running Windsor Mountain School, from which Heinz graduated in 1941. He briefly attended Wagner College, a Lutheran school on Staten Island, but was asked to leave as "an enemy alien" because the college, which overlooked the entry of New York Harbor and the Brooklyn Naval Yards, was concerned that "I might inform the Germans about ships in the harbor," said Heinz. The United States had entered World War II, with the Japanese attack on Pearl Harbor in December 1941, and as a German immigrant, Heinz was labeled a potential spy.

He left Wagner and went to Swarthmore College on a full scholarship and played on the varsity soccer team. After a half year there, Heinz volunteered for the army in 1943, initially training at Camp Ritchie (now Fort Ritchie) in Cascade, Maryland, where he was in a special military intelligence unit known as the Ritchie Boys. According to the website of the same name, and corroborated by Heinz, this unit of nine thousand mostly young, intellectual Austrian and German Jewish immigrants who had fled Nazi persecution was trained in counterintelligence, interrogation and psychological warfare because they knew the German language and psyche better than most American-born soldiers. These young men, some of whom, years later, appeared in the 2007 documentary *The Ritchie Boys*, were given the chance to help defeat an enemy that would have killed them not only for being Americans but also—in the case of most—for being born Jewish.

Heinz landed with the Ritchie Boys on Omaha Beach on D-Day, June 6, 1944, in the invasion of Normandy, just a few days after his twentieth birthday.[31] Then, after participating in the miraculous liberation of Paris and the Battle of the Bulge (his picture appears in the Lapierre and Collins book *Is Paris Burning?*, Simon and Schuster, 1965, 156), Heinz's unit crossed the Rhine in the spring of 1945 to occupy the German Ruhr Valley and to liberate the Dachau concentration camp. "Seeing Dachau made me an atheist for the rest of my life," said Heinz. For three days, he interrogated Nazi guards and other German officers, asking them, for example, about their methods for killing people and how they disposed of the bodies. He used the Ritchie Boys' interrogation technique of empathy, not violence, but noted that "it was hard not to want to murder them." These encounters with the killers of thousands of Jews "made a very strong impression," said Heinz and, suggested Pamela Esler, '74, "may understandably have left Heinz with lifelong psychological scars, what we might now call post-traumatic stress syndrome." Said Annemarie about Heinz in 2011, "He is bitter about life and about the war. He must have had a very bad experience." And Daniel Kegan, '61, now an intellectual property rights lawyer, observed, "His eyes were always sad."

Heinz was awarded a Purple Heart, having been wounded in the war, and five battle stars for bravery and service, but Eric Bondy, his younger son, said, "[My father] didn't pay attention to his Purple Heart, and he never once alluded to his experience as a Ritchie Boy." Eric found out about that part of Heinz's life only a few years ago, when he went with him to Washington for a reunion of the group. He added that Heinz also contributed to the oral history archive of the Holocaust Museum in Washington by describing both the family's escape from the Nazis and his own war experiences, including being present at the preliminary stages of the Nuremberg Trials.[32]

After returning to Swarthmore with the aid of the GI Bill of Rights, Heinz graduated in 1949 with a major in history and then completed a master's in modern European history at Bryn Mawr College, where he was one of the only male students. From the fall of 1950 to the spring of 1951, he taught at the Roeper City and Country School in Bloomfield Hills, Michigan, before going to Lenox at the age of twenty-seven to teach and take on the position of headmaster at the Windsor Mountain School after his father, Max, died. "I guess that made me the youngest headmaster in captivity," Heinz told

Stephen Rose in a February 4, 1973 *Berkshire Eagle* article titled "Windsor Mountain School—Where Students Grow."

At the behest of his mother, Gertrud, Heinz assumed the role of headmaster, but he did so reluctantly, said Franny Hall. "Heinz had thought of quite a different life." Annemarie noted, "He didn't really want to take over the school, but he felt he had to; he had no other options—nothing was pulling him elsewhere." Lesley Larsen Albert, '61, one of a handful of local Lenox students who attended Windsor and who, like her mother, Virginia, became a nurse there, remembered history teacher Donald "Duck" Daley describe how he saw Heinz as he "sat out underneath the tree in the wide expanse of the front lawn and cried, and said, 'Duck, I don't want this. She's [Gertrud] going to make me do it.' He just couldn't say no to his mother." Some faculty speculated that this inability to say no to Gertrud might have been the beginning of Heinz's difficulty in future years of saying no to people who made requests of him as headmaster—for example, when he might allow a student to leave campus on weekends despite the fact that her mother had refused to give her permission to do so (though *students* praised him for this because it showed he trusted them) or, said Larsen, "when people would call and say, 'Gee, Heinz, you know I'm short this month; I can't give you tuition,' and he'd say, 'Fine.'" Bob Blafield said that the running joke among faculty was, "Did you hear that Heinz put his foot down today…in mid-air?"

His apparent inability to say no seems also to have extended to his dogs. For example, Lesley Albert, describing one night when she was headed to Heinz and his wife, Eleanor's, house to babysit, said, "I was afraid of their dogs, so I went to one of the faculty and said, 'You gotta tell them if they want me to babysit, they gotta call off the dogs.' One time one of the dogs got a hold of my coat and ruined it. And I had black and blue marks on my arm." "There were lots of biters on campus," said Franny Hall, "but Heinz's dogs were the worst," a view substantiated by Peter Whitehead, '67,[33] who reported hearing that one of Heinz's dogs had attacked and killed a smaller dog that was with a family visiting the campus. (Fifty years later, when I went down to Maryland to interview Heinz at his home, I became the latest person—I think—to be bitten on the back of the leg by one of the three dogs he had at the time.)

Besides graduating from Swarthmore College in 1948, Heinz that year also married Eleanor Burwell, one of his classmates there and the daughter of Charles Sidney Burwell (1893–1967), the dean of Harvard Medical School from 1935 to 1949. She was described by faculty and students alike

Eleanor Bondy returning math tests to students. *From 1958 Windsor catalogue.*

as "brilliant and stunning." "Everyone loved her," said Zuzana Wiener, who added that Eleanor was "a talented and excellent teacher, head of the mathematics department and played the piano beautifully." But problems developed. When she and Heinz arrived at Windsor, Eleanor began dealing with alcoholism and spent long periods in treatment at Austen Riggs in nearby Stockbridge and the Paine Whitney Clinic in Manhattan. She made several attempts at rehab but was never able to conquer the illness.

While running the school with Heinz, Eleanor's relationship with Gertrud was tense, according to Zuzana and Daniel Kegan, because Gertrud seemed to be unwilling to give up any of her power and allow Heinz and Eleanor to manage the school together. They both believed, as did others, that that tension might have exacerbated Eleanor's alcohol problems. Heinz eventually sued for divorce, initially because of his concern, he said, about the effect Eleanor's alcoholism was having on the safety of the children (they had adopted two infants, Peter and Eric). Bob McCormick, '57, said that by the time he graduated, Eleanor, whom he greatly admired, "was getting worse." After a year's stay at Paine Whitney, during which time a graduate of Windsor Mountain, Carolyn Louks, '63, looked after the children, Eleanor returned to Windsor, but "it still wasn't working; she was hiding bottles of gin," McCormick said. After their divorce in 1965, Eleanor, "devastated by the loss of her children," moved to the eastern part of the state where her family lived. She died in 1967, the same year Heinz married Carolyn, by then a junior at Smith College. Heinz said he had initially courted Carolyn by flying to Northampton, Massachusetts, to pick her up in Howie Spaeth's ('57) plane and "flying very low to signal her" about his arrival.

After their marriage, Carolyn finished her bachelor's degree at the University of Massachusetts–Amherst and her master's at the Massachusetts Institute of Technology, after which she returned to Windsor Mountain for six years and taught freshman social studies, American history and Russian history. Roselle Van Nostrand recalled Carolyn as a serious person and remembers her holding class in her living room, where she'd sit on the radiator top and lecture. "She'd tell us, 'Coffee's on, help yourself,'" said Van Nostrand. "And as for Heinz, he was the father I never had." (By 1975, the year that Windsor Mountain closed, Carolyn had already been accepted by Boston University Medical School, from which she graduated in 1981.)

Though she admired Heinz, Jeannie Whitehead, '71, and others, described his leadership style as "laissez-faire." He "was a bit of a soft-touch," she said. "He hoped students would apply self-discipline," adding that "he wasn't much of a businessman." Music teacher Bob Blafield, confirming Jeannie's assessment, said, "Heinz didn't have a clue about money and spent a lot he didn't have. But he was a man who wanted to please, and he meant well—and he paid me a good salary. He was an empathetic man who always stood up for any student who had been wronged." Franny Hall, on the other hand, said that Heinz's concern for students sometimes went too far, as when he would excuse their behavior over a teacher's reprimand. For example, when one of her students didn't show up for her rehearsals, she said, Heinz accepted the student's "lame excuse." She added, "He needed to be loved by the kids."

Despite these comments about his leadership style, there was praise for Heinz's ability to build upon and expand the legacy of his parents. Students were grateful for the freedom he gave them to express themselves, to learn from their own mistakes and to pursue their personal passions. And further, in opening the school to a racially and economically diverse and international student body, Heinz demonstrated for them that one can truly make a difference in the world. And, indeed, an article in the *Berkshire Eagle* of February 26, 1966, indicated that Heinz's success in making Windsor Mountain an inclusive school did not go unnoticed. At the brotherhood dinner of the Berkshire Ebony Club, an African American social club in Pittsfield, Massachusetts, Heinz was honored for "his never-ending efforts in teaching students of Windsor Mountain School the rewards of growing up without aggression, free from prejudice, hatred and envy." George Roeper, too, reminded Windsor Mountain students of Heinz's belief in activism and justice. In his speech at Windsor's June 8, 1968 graduation (retrieved from The Roeper School archives), he said: "Heinz Bondy has taught you not only to be aware of the issues of today but also to do something about [them]…If peace is the issue, you are free to go out and demonstrate for it…and participate in the solutions of the problems of our time."

By the 1970s, Windsor Mountain School faced serious debt caused in part by a devastating nationwide recession, leading Heinz, then in his mid-fifties, to take the dramatic step of closing the school in 1975. It was at that point that Carolyn went to medical school in Boston, and Heinz, for the next twenty-plus years, took on several different administrative positions, the first as assistant vice-chancellor of student affairs at UMass Boston—at a time in history when students across the country were demanding a greater say in running their schools. When he was let go for "programmatic reasons," Heinz said the decision was based on his reputation as "an outspoken student advocate," according to a March 11, 1980 *Mass Media* article by Meg Hern. Students demonstrated vigorously on his behalf, but in the end, both the students and Heinz lost the fight.

Next, Heinz helped to found the Elkins Mountain School in Elkins, West Virginia, with alumnus Bob McCormick, who eventually established his own school, the Allegro School, in Claverack, New York, that McCormick described as "radically more progressive than Windsor Mountain." Heinz then went on to run the Canterbury School in Accokeek, Maryland, before ending his career in education at the age of seventy-four as headmaster from 1994 to 1998 at the Christian Family Montessori School in Mount Rainier, Maryland. In an online *Washington Post* article, "The Soul of a

The Bondy Haus, location of the Bondy archives at Schule Marienau. *Courtesy of Schule Marienau.*

School," May 4, 1996, Colman McCarthy, citing the excellence of that school under Heinz's leadership, wrote, "Heinz Bondy [believes] that parents want their children to be taught to 'adjust to the world, but not conform...'" His motto apparently continued to have a life well beyond Windsor Mountain School.

In 1999, Heinz returned to Germany—fifty years after he had attended his parents' school there—in order to attend a celebration in honor of his parents, Max and Gertrud, organized by Wolf-Dieter Hasenclever, the liberal headmaster of Schule Marienau from 1986 to 1999 and the first of the school's administrators to take the step of doing research on the school's Jewish founders. He also established the Bondy Haus and archives at the school in 1989. Now an education consultant in Berlin, Hasenclever noted that "the school remains proud of the Bondys' pedagogical roots."

Heinz Bondy died on February 18, 2014, at the age of eighty-nine, at the Wilson Healthcare Center in Gaithersburg, Maryland, after a short battle with cancer, having years earlier survived Nazi Germany, World War II and two heart operations. Surviving Heinz are two sons, Eric and Peter; four grandchildren; and his wife, Dr. Carolyn Bondy.

When I asked Heinz about his own legacy, he replied, "Maybe I helped somebody who wouldn't have done as well without me." And dozens of students testified that he did. Soon after Peter Bondy posted his father's obituary on Facebook on February 19, 2014, alumni posted loving tributes about how Heinz had saved their lives, how he had trusted them, forgiven them, advised them, provided them with a safe haven, taught them about social justice and inspired them to want to make the world a better place. Among the tributes was one by Thelonius Sphere Monk Jr., '69, who wrote:

> *Heinz and Gertrud were like my de facto parents…and I was a very bad boy a lot of the time. Despite my recalcitrant attitude, I learned. Both academically and spiritually. The family were brilliant educators, and I am eternally grateful. The world always misses the likes of a Heinz Bondy. RIP, Mr. Bondy.*

CURT WERNER BONDY (1894–1972)

While Curt Bondy, a younger brother of Max and a cousin of Gertrud's, is not directly associated with Windsor Mountain School, his life portrays another setting in which the Bondy philosophy of education changed the lives of young people in profound ways.

Curt Bondy was a charismatic psychologist and teacher, as well as a hero during the early stages of the Nazi Holocaust, the term that refers to the systematic murder of six million Jews and millions of others by the Nazis and their collaborators that began in earnest in 1938 and ended with the conclusion of World War II in 1945. As director of the Gross Breesen Agricultural Training Camp, he helped to save the lives of dozens of German Jewish teenagers by making it possible for them to acquire the skills that would enable them to emigrate to locations around the world. Of the 173 young men and women who passed through the farm school between 1936 and 1941, some 158 were able to leave Nazi Germany and almost certain death behind them.

The agricultural trainees at Gross Breesen (pronounced Bray-sen) benefitted from Bondy's curriculum at the school, which included

Curt Bondy, director of the farm school at the Gross Breesen Agricultural Training Camp, Germany, 1937. *From the* Circular Letters.

farming skills, affirmation of Jewish tradition and an appreciation of the aspects of German culture that transcended "the pollution of Nazi ideology and practice."[34]

Prior to organizing the "Final Solution," their genocidal plan for the Jews, the Nazis initially tried to find ways to encourage them to leave Germany. And after the passage of the Nuremberg Laws in 1935, the Nazi government began to explore ways to provide an orderly exodus of Jews, especially the young. One of those ways was to allow the Central

Association of German Jews to establish an emigration training farm for boys and girls between the ages of fifteen and twenty-three, whose ultimate destination would be countries other than Israel, then Palestine. (All of the other training farms were Zionist-based and prepared the young Jews to emigrate to Palestine.) The result was the founding of the Gross Breesen Agricultural Training Camp, where Curt Bondy was selected as director by, among others, Rabbi Dr. Leo Baeck (1873–1956), scholar and leader of Progressive Judaism, and Martin Buber (1878–1965), Jewish humanist and theologian and a friend of Bondy's.[35]

Curt Werner Bondy was born in Hamburg on January 17, 1894, and attended Schloss Bischofsstein, a private school, where he came into contact with the German Youth Movement, of which both he and his brother, Max, were ardent followers as well as leaders. With the onset of World War I in 1914, he was prevented from continuing his study of medicine and instead served on the Western Front in the German Medical Corps.

After working in the area of reform for juvenile offenders, he earned his doctorate in psychology in 1926 from Hamburg University and became a social psychology professor in 1930 at Gottingen, a position he lost in 1933 "because he was a Jew." That same year, he founded the Jewish Center for Adult Education in Frankfurt am Main with Martin Buber, and three years later, he was appointed director of the Gross Breesen Farm School.

By May 1936, the first trainees arrived at the training camp,[36] which, like Schule Marienau, was rooted in the traditions of the German Boarding School Movement and the German Youth Movement and emphasized character-building education. For example, every night at the farm camp, Curt, or "Herr Bo," as he was affectionately called, held "Knowing Life" sessions, or *lebenskunde*, where students learned about ideas similar to those that Max shared in his "Talks to Students": "Live consciously. Be responsible. Look out for one another." A former trainee at Gross Breesen, Werner Angress, remembered one of Curt's main themes, self-awareness, or *bewusstmachung*, what today might be referred to as "consciousness-raising."[37]

While overseeing the academic program as well as recreational and farming activities, Curt was, at the same time, working anxiously on locating placements abroad for his trainees. And by the summer of 1939, his efforts met with success in an extraordinary breakthrough dubbed "The Virginia Plan," which helped to secure visas for approximately twenty-one Gross Breeseners, thus enabling them to become part of the Hyde Farmlands experiment (1938–41). Modeled on Gross Breesen, it was established with the generosity of Richmond department store owner William Thalhimer and his cousin Morton, who, in 1938, purchased 1,500 acres of farmland in Burkeville, Virginia, a few hours south of Richmond. Hyde Farmlands would become the American Gross Breesen, a safe haven and a work and education site for the young Gross Breeseners.[38]

But the trainees still in Germany did not fare as well. Between the time of Curt's visit to the United States in the spring of 1938 to help establish the Virginia Plan and the summer of 1939, when the twenty-one visas were secured, the pogrom known as *Kristallnacht*, or "The Night of Broken Glass"—considered the real beginning of the Holocaust—exploded on November 9 and 10, 1938, and with it came the demise of Gross Breesen. Bondy had already returned to the training farm when SS men drove onto the property; arrested all the male trainees eighteen and older and staff members, including Curt; and imprisoned them in the Buchenwald concentration camp for a month (November–December 1938). They were, however, among the more fortunate since, with the help of relatives, friends and various service agencies, they were spared further persecution and freed. However, the trainees who remained at Gross Breesen were unable to leave, and on August 31, 1941, the farm school was terminated by the Gestapo and the remaining trainees reduced to forced laborers. All were eventually deported and ultimately murdered in the Holocaust, most of them in Auschwitz.[39]

With assistance from the New York Jewish Joint Distribution Committee, Curt arrived in New York on August 21, 1940, and thereafter divided his time between Richmond, where he taught at a branch of William and Mary College, and the farm at Hyde Farmlands, which ended up closing in 1941. The young Breeseners spread out all over the world but continued to stay in touch with one another through their *Circular Letters* or *Rundbriefe*, initiated by Curt in 1936 and now available online.[40]

Curt moved back to Germany in 1950 when he was offered the William Stern Chair of the Psychology Department of Hamburg University, remaining in that position until his retirement in 1959. His grandnephew Tom Roeper noted that Curt was upset about the Nazis who were still very much alive and working there but that "he actually got along with them." As president of the Professional Association of German Psychologists, Curt lectured throughout Europe and never stopped looking for ways to save the lives of young people. For example, upon his return to Germany, he created an organization for the multiracial, illegitimate children left behind by black soldiers.[41]

Annemarie, Curt's niece, wrote: "We all knew he was gay, and he had a boyfriend for many years that I knew well and liked."[42] In our conversation, she expressed love and admiration for her uncle and spoke of his contributions to the world as a psychologist, humanitarian, prolific author, charismatic educator and hero. "Curt was the star of the family," she told me.

Curt Bondy, "Herr Bo," died in January 1972 and was mourned by Gross Breeseners all across the globe, who, despite their being uprooted by the Nazis, were, with Curt's help, able to survive and even flourish in new environments. He is buried in Hamburg.

Jan Gerhardt "Gerdi" Wiener (1920–2010)

Gerdi Wiener was both a "fighter," who literally battled with many enemies during his life, and an inspiring teacher. "Just watching [Jan] talking or teaching with young people was beauty itself," said Jan Urban, a friend of Gerdi's and a journalist in Prague.[43]

After suffering a stroke in 2009, Jan was unable to return to the Berkshires and his home in Lenox, Massachusetts, as he and Zuzana, his wife, had always done after one or two semesters teaching Czech history and language to students in study abroad programs offered by American University and New York University. Instead, he spent nearly a year and a half dying in a Prague military hospital. "He held court there," said Zuzana, among visiting friends like the former Czech president Vaclev Havel (1936–2011), whom he had helped to elect after the Czech Republic's transition from communism to democracy in 1989, and among Havel's friends, including folksinger and activist Joan Baez, who, according to Zuzana, said to Jan, "You rascal, what are you doing here?" and then sang to him in Spanish.

Before coming to Windsor Mountain School to teach in 1964, Jan Wiener's life reads like fiction. He had survived first the Nazis and then the communists by sheer luck and use of his physical prowess. A 1998 documentary about Jan titled *The Fighter*, directed by Emir Bar-Lev, shows an older Jan retracing the steps of his life with his friend Arnost Lustig and looking much like he always did, sporting "the same old country mustache like the handlebars on a racing bike" and silver hair "with the sun...making it glisten like alpine snow"—words that author Gerry Hausman used to describe a character in his book *Night Flight* whom he modeled after Jan.[44] Hausman considered Jan a mentor and friend while they were both teachers at Windsor Mountain.

Folksinger Joan Baez (left) with Zuzana Wiener and Jan "Gerdi" Wiener, teachers at Windsor Mountain. *Courtesy of Zuzana Wiener.*

In a conversation broadcast on **WAMC** Northeast Public Radio in 2008, Jan described his unusual life story, beginning with his birth on May 26, 1920, in Hamburg, to which his parents had moved after World War I and where his father, Julius, or Jula, Gertrud Bondy's brother, had set up a pharmaceutical import-export firm. He was a liberal Jew who, as Jan said, knew writers Franz Kafka and Franz Werfel. And Jan proudly said that his grandfather had been an orthodox rabbi.

The Wieners were living in Hamburg when Hitler came to power in 1933. Seeing the writing on the wall, Julius took the family back to Prague. But soon after Jan graduated from the gymnasium in Prague in 1939, the Nazis marched into Czechoslovakia. At that point, his father and stepmother fled to Yugoslavia, with Jan following in 1941, in hopes of getting a visa to England and then to the United States. But on April 6, 1941, the Germans entered Yugoslavia as well, and Julius, desperate and tired of running—and believing there was no way out—decided to commit suicide by taking poison; his second wife did the same. Jan described how, just prior to his father's suicide, Julius said to him, "I choose to take the last of my freedom—to die in my own way." (Jan's mother, Franciska, had died in Terezin (Teresienstadt), a concentration camp north of Prague, in February 1942.)

Jan then fled to Italy, where he learned from resistance fighters how he could escape by riding under a train, which he did, cramped into a tiny space for eighteen hours upside down on a steel plate, until he arrived in Genoa, where he was caught by the Italian police and sent to a medieval Italian prison for political prisoners for nine and a half months. After numerous solitary confinements and escapes (1942–43) in different locations, he encountered British soldiers, who had just freed Italy from the fascists. Given the option, Jan decided to join the Czech division of the British Air Force in Wales, where he trained as a navigator, serving in the 311 Bomber Squad until the end of the war.[45] Because he spoke fluent German, he was also asked to act as interpreter for General Josef Burtik, one of the leading officers of Czechoslovak Intelligence in Great Britain and the chief organizer of the plot to assassinate Reinhard Heydrich, a major architect of the Holocaust. That plot was the subject of Jan's 1969 book, *The Assassination of Heydrich*.

With the end of the war, Jan was able to return to Prague, where he was both a student at Charles University and a teacher of English—that is, until the Czechoslovak communist coup d'état in 1948. Because he refused to join the party and because the anti-Nazi fighters who had fought in the West were considered enemies of the communist state, Wiener was arrested and spent five and a half years in a communist prison.[46] Finally, in 1955, he was allowed to return to Prague, where he became an instructor in the language department of the Research Institute for Technical High Schools.

In the years that followed, Jan's aunt Gertrud Bondy and his brother, Tom Winner (who had changed his name from Wiener), tried to help Jan get out of communist Czechoslovakia by writing letters to Eleanor Roosevelt, who had been instrumental in organizing immigration assistance for those seeking to leave communist countries, just as she had done earlier for refugees fleeing from Nazi Germany. Annemarie Bondy Roeper, Jan's cousin, said in an interview with this author that Gertrud was the first of the family to connect with Mrs. Roosevelt, "maybe through psychoanalysts in the U.S. or her friendship with Freud." Said Annemarie, "Mrs. Roosevelt helped us to get to the U.S., and I came to know her through my mother."

The Roepers invited Eleanor Roosevelt to speak at their school on October 3, 1957, and Tom Roeper, then thirteen, remembered meeting her that day. More importantly, soon after that visit, a correspondence between Roosevelt and Jan's family began in their efforts to get him out of communist Czechoslovakia.

When, during his interview on Northeast Public Radio, Jan referred to a letter he received from Mrs. Roosevelt, I became curious about whether this or any other letters might still exist. I wrote to Sarah Malcolm, archivist at the Franklin D. Roosevelt Presidential Library in Hyde Park, New York,[47] and she responded in a February 23, 2011 e-mail, saying that she had found a treasure-trove of "letters exchanged between Thomas Winner [Jan's brother] and Eleanor Roosevelt from 1957 to 1959." The collection revealed the complex negotiations that had been involved in securing permission for Jan to leave Czechoslovakia. In the earliest of Winner's letters to Roosevelt, dated October 17, 1957, just two weeks after Roosevelt spoke at The Roeper School, and typed on Duke University stationery, he wrote:

> *May I thank you with all my heart for a very kind action which my cousin-in-law, George Roeper...has just written me you are taking. In his letter my cousin said that you wrote him you would write a letter to my brother, Jan G. Wiener, in Prague in order to help him to emigrate to the West. It gives one renewed faith in humanity to think of the action you are willing to take for a victim of persecution who you do not at all know.*

In another letter dated November 22, 1958, and written from Ann Arbor, Michigan, where Winner had taken a university position, he wrote:

> *Dear Mrs. Roosevelt,*
>
> *May I, however inadequately, thank you again for your great kindness to me and to my brother, Jan Wiener, in Czechoslovakia. I was so happy to have been able to meet you at the University of Michigan after your speech there.*

Winner then goes on to make the case for Jan's need of her assistance.

Gertrud Bondy's letter to Mrs. Roosevelt, dated August 25, 1959, and typed on Windsor Mountain stationery, expressed her thanks to Roosevelt "for the wonderful and generous help that you have given to my nephew, Gerhard Jan Wiener in Prague. I know that it was life-saving for him. I know that you are still continuing to help him, and I am extremely grateful to you."

Jan wrote to Roosevelt from his brother's home in Ann Arbor on June 26, 1960, to let her know that he had, indeed, made his way successfully to the United States, thanks to her help. During his stay, Jan was also able to visit Gertrud at Windsor Mountain School.

In another letter, Mrs. Roosevelt invited Jan to her home for lunch on July 17, 1960, and Jan responded on July 6, 1960: "We will be at Val-

WINDSOR MOUNTAIN SCHOOL
LENOX, MASSACHUSETTS

August 25, 1959

Trans

Mrs. Franklin Roosevelt
Hyde Park,
New York

Dear Mrs. Roosevelt:

      I don't know whether you remember me, I
met you only once. But I am a very old friend of
Dorothy Canfield Fisher, whose death was a great
loss for me.

      I am writing to you today to thank you
for your wonderful and generous help that you have
given to my nephew, Gerhard Jan Wiener in Prague.
I know that it was lifesaving for him. I know
you are still continuing to help him and I am
extremely grateful to you. I hope that he will
be able to emigrate and that he will live here
next year and teach in our school.

      My brother's two boys lived with me
for a long time and I consider them as my own
children.

      I wish to express besides my thanks,
my great admiration and respect that I have
always had for you and President Roosevelt.

               Very devotedly yours,

               Gertrud Bondy

               Dr. Gertrud Bondy
               Principal

GB:ms
enc.

P.S. I am sending you a catalog of our school,
    under separate cover, so that you will
    know something about it.

Letter from Gertrud Bondy to Eleanor Roosevelt, 1959. *Courtesy of the Franklin D. Roosevelt Presidential Library.*

Kill cottage [on July 17] at 1:00 p.m." Jan, who went alone to the lunch, described his visit with Mrs. Roosevelt in some detail in his radio interview: "She [Mrs. Roosevelt] took me by the hand and brought me to her study and asked me about my life. During the lunch, she put her hand on mine and asked, 'Do you like the meal?' And I told her, 'I think it is delicious.' Then she said to me, 'Tell it to Doris [Roosevelt's African American servant].' And I did."

Jan had met Zuzana Hloczek in Prague in 1957, when he moved into her family's home. She was then thirteen and he thirty-seven. Six years later, she became his third wife, and in 1964, they came to the United States, having finally been given permission by the Czech government to leave. Zuzana said that Jan's two sons from an earlier marriage, Michael and Daniel, came later, in 1967 or 1968, with the Russian invasion of Prague. Both boys eventually graduated from Windsor Mountain School. (Jan and Zuzana later had two children together, Joe and Tanya.) Zuzana's brother, Peter, also came to Windsor Mountain from Czechoslovakia in 1968, when the Soviets invaded that country, and many Windsor students remember him teaching them mathematics using visual methods because he had not yet learned English.

Both Jan and Zuzana started teaching at Windsor Mountain in 1964, a case of "nepotism," he admitted, since his aunt and uncle, Gertrud and Max, had founded the school. And, indeed, there were episodes when Jan used his relationship to Gertrud in "very hurtful ways," according to Franny Hall, who was on the receiving end of some of these episodes.

While Jan could be a controversial figure, he was also a popular teacher, according to Jeannie Whitehead, '71, a student in his modern European history course, who said, "I felt privileged to be taught by someone who had lived the history he was teaching," a statement repeated by many other alumni. Physical fitness being his major preoccupation, Jan also taught calisthenics and *sokol*, Czech for "falcon," a form of Czech gymnastics from the nineteenth century, often done outdoors, with weights and poles. Students recalled seeing Jan on the lawn early every morning as he engaged in his daily exercise routine. And every now and then, he'd yell out to them to come join him, and a few of them did.

Bob Blafield, the one-man music department, considered Jan a friend but called him "an old-fashioned male chauvinist. He could be abusive. And I never knew what was true with Jan. He always exaggerated. On the other hand, he was a great mentor to the kids, and physically, he was an inspiration. He could ski all the way to the top of Mount Greylock [the highest mountain in Massachusetts]. But then he would always brag about it."

Tom Roeper, Jan's cousin, wrote: "Gerdi was lively and popular, but he was the rough, tough John Wayne type. He felt he should be assistant principal, but he was much too authoritarian, which Heinz knew and so did everyone else."

Zuzana commented on these conflicting views of her husband: "Well, they found him, you know, very controversial, and I think they loved him and hated him in some ways because he asked for discipline…because [students] didn't have any discipline in their lives, and very often it's because the parents don't give them borders, and they're asking for [them]."

When Windsor Mountain School closed in 1975, Jan taught briefly at nearby Stockbridge School, as did several of his colleagues, but that school closed, too, less than a year later. That's when Zuzana and Jan went to a school in Sedona, Arizona, where they taught for five years (1975–80), followed by another five years (1980–85) at a school in Baden, Württemberg, Germany.

They returned to Lenox, Massachusetts, in 1985, when Jan was sixty-five, and for the next four years, he taught, lectured and worked at several venues in the Berkshires until a world-changing event occurred: the collapse of communism in 1989. This led to the opportunity for Zuzana and Jan to return to Prague, where Jan campaigned for Vaclev Havel, Czech playwright, poet and philosopher, and ultimately helped him to get elected as the first president of the Czech Republic (1993–2003). It was during his time campaigning for Havel that Jan started teaching a course at Charles University, which led to both Zuzana and Jan becoming part of the faculty in two study abroad programs in Prague. When they would return to Lenox each summer, both were employed by Canyon Ranch, a luxurious spa, where they led activities in the Department of Outdoor Sports.

In 2001, Vaclev Havel awarded Jan the Medal of Merits of First Degree at Prague Castle's Vladislav Hall for his contributions to his native country, where he continued to lecture until his eighty-eighth birthday in 2008. Soon after that, Jan had a stroke and entered the hospital in Prague, where he died in 2010 at the age of ninety.

Jan referred to himself as the "Wandering Jew," and before he died, he asked Zuzana to spread his ashes in the seven places he loved most, among them, the grounds of Windsor Mountain School. Ashes were also spread at Mountainview Cemetery, where Jan's gravestone stands close to that of his aunt and uncle, Gertrud and Max.

Václav Havel (left), first president of the Czech Republic, with Jan Wiener, history teacher at Windsor Mountain School. *Courtesy of Zuzana Wiener.*

Though Jan lost most of his family in the Nazi Holocaust, his older brother, Tom Winner, survived. He had received a scholarship to Harvard University in 1939, under a program for refugees, and, after graduating from Schule Marienau, was able to find his way out of Nazi-occupied Prague. A respected scholar and professor, Winner died in 2004.[48] Both his wife and two daughters are educators, and daughter Ellen is married to Dr. Howard Gardner, a Harvard research psychologist and professor known for his theory of multiple intelligences.

Jan's wife, Zuzana, continues to teach in Prague in two study abroad programs.

Chapter 2

The 1920s and '30s: A Humanistic Philosophy Evolves Out of Trauma: The Bondys Flee from Nazis and Reestablish Their School in America

Because of the atmosphere at Marienau, human beings have learned a touch more love, more trust. [T]hat is the most important experience that they have gained. They are now a shade more open and humane.
—Max Bondy, 1937[49]

MAX AND GERTRUD ESTABLISH THEIR PHILOSOPHY AND THEIR FIRST SCHOOL

In reference to the location of Max and Gertrud's first permanent school, their daughter, Annemarie, wrote:

> *Old farms were scattered around the landscape* [where] *many people kept beehives and made heather honey. Somehow in the middle of all this was the farm called Marienau, which was a rather big piece of property stretching over 300 acres. It originally consisted of one main building—a white stucco farmhouse with a red-tiled roof—where my family and some of the students lived. Later, the surrounding stables were converted into classrooms, dormitories and single rooms. It was there that my parents continued to develop their idealistic school community and boarding school.*[50]

Before moving to Marienau in the spring of 1929, the Bondys had opened their Free School and Work Community (1920–23) in a former hotel, Sintalhof, in Bruckenau. Then, after parting ways with co-founder Ernst Putz, they moved the school to Gandersheim, a beautiful historic town with cobblestone streets, where they rented a former hospital and opened School Community Gandersheim (1923–29), all made possible with an early inheritance from Max's father, Siegfried.[51]

Schule Marienau, named for the village in which it was located, was established at a time when several dramatic movements were beginning to cause excitement within German educational circles. The German Youth Movement (1896–1933), the German Boarding School Movement and the progressive education movement of the early twentieth century all played a role in the development of Max Bondy's philosophy—along with one other influence, said his friend Ernst Cramer: "Both Max and [his brother] Curt had been shaped by two experiences: 1) the youth movement [and] 2) the First World War. The result of this for both [was] the disapproval of the war, but also the spirit for comradeship and a very critical attitude towards the bourgeois way of life. They also brought home the courage to have a positive attitude in all vicissitudes of life."[52]

These views developed despite—or maybe because of—the fact that their brother Walter was killed in the war, and Max himself was wounded and thereafter walked with a limp. The lofty spirit of the German Youth Movement with its slogan, "To run our own lives according to our decisions, responsible to ourselves and in absolute truth," prevailed at both Schule Marienau and, later, the Windsor Mountain School, where it became the foundation for democratic practices like the student government and court, and also at Gross Breesen, the agricultural school where Curt was director. Embracing romantic ideals like a return to nature and living an adventurous life, the German Youth Movement had developed as a form of protest, its members depressed by society's conventions, artificiality and materialism, and its absence of human warmth and sincerity.[53] Believing that the movement's devotion to freedom, clean living and healthy outdoor activities could change student culture in Germany—at that time characterized by drinking, dueling, sexual promiscuity and alienation—Max and Curt Bondy became followers and eventually leaders within the movement. Annemarie Bondy Roeper, who grew up at Schule Marienau, noted in her memoir that one of the movement's many "healthy outdoor" pastimes, folk-dancing, was *her* favorite. "The girls dressed in long flowing skirts and didn't wear make-up," she wrote. And above all, there was no double standard. The youth movement believed in equality of the sexes.[54]

"Wandering Bird," or *Wandervogel*, symbol of the German Youth Movement. *Wikipedia.*

Most appealing to Max, however, was the movement's zeal for mountain climbing and hiking, referred to as rambling, or *wandervogel* in German, meaning "wandering bird." This is the image that came to represent the youth movement and its central principle: valuing community (*gemeinschaft*) without sacrificing one's individual identity, Max's mantra.[55] Building community—*real* caring about and respect for one another—was the foundation for every school the Bondys created. Everyone counted.

When he came to power in 1933, Hitler abolished the youth movement and put in its place Hitler Youth, which, unlike its predecessor, was fiercely nationalistic and militaristic and required obedience to Nazi dogma. However, anti-Semitism and a passion for German national traditions had taken root earlier within several branches of the youth movement, and Hitler's aims might have been facilitated by the earlier existence of such a movement.

Another influence on Max Bondy was the Landerziehungsheime, or the German Country Boarding School Movement, that arose at the end of the nineteenth century and continued through the first third of the twentieth, its origins residing in the progressive education movement, or the *neue padagogik* (new pedagogy). Herman Lietz (1868–1919) founded the first such boarding school in 1898 and was soon joined by other alternative educationists—referred to in Germany as "reform pedagogues"—including Max Bondy, Paul Geheeb (1870–1961), Martin Luserke (1880–1968), Gustav Wyneken (1875–1964), Kurt Hahn (1886–1974) and Rudolf Steiner (1861–1925), all of whom had been influenced by the German Youth Movement.

Lietz had based his school on an English model, Abbotsholme, founded by Cecil Reddie, which emphasized sports and crafts along with modern languages. Rote learning and classical languages were de-emphasized, as was class privilege. And while the pioneers of these country boarding schools might have differed in terms of, say, their devotion to physical performance (which was a priority, for example, for Kurt Hahn, a German Jew and founder of the "Salem System" and the Outward Bound Program), they all believed that goals such as student participation, service to society, formation of character and a co-educational, international environment could lead to a complete transformation of society.[56]

In the early part of the twentieth century, progressives like Max Bondy were responding to the growth of industrialization and its accompanying social changes, including government-funded schools, where standardized mass education was being offered in factory-like conditions. These developments made it difficult for teachers to address children's individual needs and interests, the major focus of these child-centered pioneers.

Max's traumatic war experience also led to his belief that boarding schools, equipped with psychological knowledge, were the best environment for "educating the child's emotions," which are "easier to educate…within the framework of a group than within that of a family," said Max in a speech at the Yale Institute for Mental Health (date unclear) and published later in Windsor Mountain's 1955 yearbook. Interestingly, in one of their talks with students, Gertrud said that their support for student self-government was *not* primarily a method to educate them about democracy but "much more important, to give their charged emotions a new direction."

In particular, Max thought that children needed help in dealing with their natural aggressive drives. Neither Max nor Gertrud agreed with the harsh punishment they saw in German public schools as the method for dealing with those drives. Rather, personal talks and trying to find out the reasons behind such behavior were, they believed, more likely to bring about change. It's clear that Gertrud influenced Max, who at first did not recognize her background in psychology as vital to his philosophy.

Many of Germany's urban elementary teachers were also part of the progressive education movement.[57] Marjorie Lamberti, professor emerita of history at Middlebury College, noted that many of them had read John

Dewey's (1859–1952) early work and were aware that his principles could be traced back to reformers of the past, like Johann Heinrich Pestalozzi (1746–1827), a Swiss humanist; Johann Friedrich Herbart (1776–1841), a German philosopher and psychologist; and Friedrich Froebel (1782–1852), father of the kindergarten.[58] Dewey himself had been influenced by these pioneers as well as the new pedagogues while a graduate student at Johns Hopkins, where one of his professors was the experimental psychologist G. Stanley Hall, who had just returned from studying with the leaders of reform in Germany.[59]

THE NEW PEDAGOGY AT SCHULE MARIENAU

In her memoir, Annemarie Bondy Roeper describes at length how her parents put into practice at Schule Marienau a new pedagogy that encouraged learning "by doing" and honored the philosophies of their historic forbears. They held assemblies where everyone had a voice; there were sports of all kinds, as well as gymnastics and hiking; and there was lots of music. Mornings began with a Bach concerto. There was also a chorus and an orchestra, and "art was everywhere," with students painting, sculpting, weaving and working with wood. And there was lots of "very lively" dancing. Classes were held both indoors and outside, as were festivals and "lots of plays," according to Annemarie, including *A Midsummer Night's Dream*. There was also time for meditation and philosophical discussion. "It was a very physical as well as intellectual life," said Annemarie, with everyone taking part in the community.[60] And although it wasn't one of the practices prescribed by the new pedagogy, she noted that "everybody smoked cigarettes," a very popular pastime at Windsor Mountain as well.

George Roeper, who had met his future wife, Annemarie Bondy, when he was a student at Schule Marienau, recalled its liberal arts–related curriculum in a speech he gave at Windsor Mountain's June 1968 graduation (retrieved from The Roeper School archives): "When I was in Max Bondy's high school forty years ago, we read Franz Kafka, and we read Freud [and] listened to Bach concertos and became acquainted with great artists like Paul Klee, Picasso, Kandinsky [and] architects like Marcel Breuer, Gropius [and] Corbusier."

Max also introduced students to jazz, which, at that time in the early '30s, was labeled "degenerate" by Hitler. Michael Kater mentions Max Bondy and Schule Marienau in his book about the place of jazz in the

'30s under the Nazis: "[Wealthy] parents sent their children to famous schools like Marienau, directed until the Nuremberg Blood Laws [1935] by a polyglot humanist, the Hamburg Jew Max Bondy."[61] Kater noted that during the Weimar Republic (1919–33), Max encouraged among his pupils an appreciation of jazz and atonal music, as well as modern art from the Bauhaus school. Said Annemarie, "The American influence was great at that time, and my Father was quite taken by it. He installed 'American Evening,' where we would discuss American authors. We were big fans of Al Jolson's rendition of 'Old Man River' and jazz music in general."[62]

The Nazis "Intervene," and the Bondys Flee

With Hitler's election as chancellor of Germany in 1933, Nazi influence began to be felt at the school as it was in all aspects of society. And by 1935, the Nazis' presence was visible at Schule Marienau. "Every morning," wrote Annemarie, "we were forced to start the day by saying, 'Heil Hitler,' followed then by our usual Bach concerto. Soon the Nazi flag was being flown over the school,"[63] and a curriculum geared toward Nazi doctrine was imposed. "There was one song I will never forget," said Annemarie. "The title of it was 'When Jewish Blood Springs from the Knife, We Will be Happy.'"[64]

Tom Roeper, Max and Gertrud's grandson and Annemarie's son, wrote, "The school was forced to have a Hitler Youth. My father [George] was forced to be a member, and Heinz, only twelve or thirteen then, said the only thing he really disliked was not being allowed to play soccer, since Hitler Youth controlled it." As a Jew, albeit converted, Heinz was not allowed to participate. Tom continued:

> *The Gestapo did raid the school—not sure of the year, maybe 1934—looking for evidence that* [the Bondys] *had left-wing sympathies. And the story was that they carefully went through Max's desk. Meanwhile, all of the suspect documents were in Gertrud's desk, and she quickly took them and flushed them down the toilet when the Gestapo was in a different part of the house.*

At first, Jews were prohibited from teaching Aryan children but not technically prevented from being the heads of schools, so Max was able to

Max Bondy with students on his last day at Schule Marienau in 1937 as Nazis officially take over his school. *Courtesy of the Roeper family*.

remain there after Hitler's election. Also, according to Annemarie, there was a high-ranking Nazi official, a friend of Hermann Goering's wife, whose daughter, a difficult teenager, came to Marienau because "they were told that the only person who could help the child was my mother [Gertrud]. This protected us for four years." But then a document came to Max that said that a person of Jewish descent wasn't fit to work with Aryan children, and "my parents were informed they had to give up the school."[65]

"My father thought at first that Hitler's dominance was a passing phase, but when it became clear what the Nazis had in mind, he fell into a deep depression and began to suffer from a terrible blood illness."[66]

In 1937, the year Annemarie graduated from Schule Marienau, Max Bondy was forced to hand over his school to Dr. Bernhard Knoop, a conservative educator appointed to officially run the school, which he did until 1969. It's not clear if Knoop was a member of the Nazi Party, but Tom Roeper admits that Knoop did have to make compromises to please the Nazis. Marienau was sold to Knoop for 180,000 marks (about $448,200 at the time), but after penalties and other maneuvers in the process of forcing Jews to sell their property to Aryans, the Bondys basically ended up with nothing.[67]

Interestingly, despite Dr. Knoop's conservatism, he was married first to Angelika Probst and then to Anneliese Graf, both of whom had family members with strong ties to the anti-Nazi resistance movement, the White Rose Society.[68]

ECOLE INTERNATIONAL DE LES RAYONS, THE BONDYS' SCHOOL IN SWITZERLAND

Unlike Max, Gertrud did not believe that Hitler was a passing phase. She left for Switzerland with Heinz and Ulla in 1936, one year before Max and Annemarie, and started a new school in Gland, on Lake Geneva, with the help of Harald Baruschke, one of their Schule Marienau alumni.[69] Wrote Gertrud in her *Personal History*, "We took some of the children with us and...[Max later] brought some children whose parents were against the Hitler regime." And there were also Jewish children whose parents had been put in concentration camps.

At Les Rayons, the ideal of community education begun at Marienau continued, and the teachers and even the youngest of the students had a voice in the running of the school. Annemarie wrote, "And with the Nazi threat and terror spreading throughout Europe, [my parents'] humanistic philosophy took on an even greater sense of urgency."[70]

At the end of their first year in Switzerland, the Bondys issued the "Report of the Ecole, Les Rayons, Gland, December, 1938," which included over twenty-five "Extracts from the Diary of a Pupil" about school life there. For example:

> *4.9.38. Morning music and morning talk.*
>
> *6.9.38. A lecture on the History of Art was given in the evening. Mr. Bondy gave a short summary of the architecture of the churches of Germany.*
>
> *17.9.38. Mr. Oppliger's group started on a three day's [sic] bicycling excursion.*
>
> *13.11.38. Mr. Bondy made a speech explaining why we were celebrating this [Autumn] Festival. He said, "We live in a world full of hatred and envy, but we, ourselves, will be free from grudge." Our festive day ended with cake eating and we all went to bed happy and content.*

The Bondys ended their report with these words:

> *We shall open a similar school in the United States at the beginning of the next year,* [the Windsor Mountain School.] *It will be run according to the same principles as our Swiss school* [and Marienau]. *An exchange of pupils should be of interest to American and Continental parents.*

Their original intent in founding Windsor Mountain School was to serve as "an American counterpart" to their Swiss school, but due to the war, they had to give up that idea. For while it seemed at first that Les Rayons was a safe haven, far away from the looming war, it soon became clear to the Bondys that this was not the case. "When we felt that a big European War was inevitable," Gertrud wrote in her memoir, "we decided to go to the United States," which they did in 1939, while Baruschke stayed on and continued running the school for a few more years.

"WINDSOR MOUNTAIN SCHOOL TO BE FOUNDED..."

George Roeper had gone to the United States earlier to find a location where the Bondys could start another school, and he found Juniper Hill Farm, in Windsor, Vermont. In the September 7, 1939 issue of the *Vermont Journal* (a weekly that ran from 1783 to around 1964), an article appeared about the Bondys' arrival in Windsor, titled "Windsor Mountain School to Be Founded at Former Evarts Home":

> *The Juniper Hill Farm owned by Mrs. Katherine Evarts of New York City has been leased for the coming year to Dr. and Mrs. Max Bundy* [sic] *and Mr. and Mrs. George Roeper of Switzerland, who will found in this beautiful location the Windsor Mountain School...Dr. and Mrs. Bundy will act as presidents of the school...As Dr. Bundy spoke of her school in Switzerland, a shadow of sadness fell over her face. "The children are enrolled and waiting," she said pensively, "but the teachers have been called to le militaire."* [The Bondys] *are friends of Dorothy Thompson*

The Juniper Inn in Windsor, Vermont, the first location of Windsor Mountain School in America. *Courtesy of TripAdvisor.*

69

and Sinclair Lewis, and Mr. and Mrs. Lewis came with them to Windsor
a short time ago to inspect the school location…Windsor and Vermont
will wish [them] *outstanding success…in this new venture…Their*
residence in the community will prove a distinct and valuable addition to
the educational and cultural life of Vermont.[71]

In their "Report for October 1939 to May 1940," in the *Second Bulletin*
of the Windsor Mountain School, issued from Windsor, Vermont, Max and
Gertrud wrote,

> *We opened the school October 1, 1939, with three students* [Heinz,
> their son; the cook's child; and Winnetou Zuckmayer] *and five*
> *teachers…We now have seven children and six new enrollments for the next*
> *year. Since we have received more applications, we expect to begin the fall*
> [1940] *term with fifteen children.*

After one year, 1939–40, they left Juniper Hill Farm and reopened
in the fall of 1940 in Manchester, Vermont, where they would stay for
four years (1940–44) and where they would continue their humanistic
educational mission.

Chapter 3

The 1940s: Windsor Mountain School in a Decade of Transitions, Geographical and Psychological

It is quite possible to live in a boarding school and yet not have the feeling of belonging to a community. Our school is, in a sense, a ship. Everyone must realize that the smooth sailing of our craft depends upon him. You are not passengers; you are working crew.
—*Max Bondy, from the "Address at the Beginning of School," published in the* Third Bulletin, *November 1940, Manchester, Vermont*

The decade of the 1940s saw a number of transitions for the Bondys as they kept afloat their practice of humanistic education. There were, for example, the geographical transitions when the school moved from Windsor, Vermont, to Manchester and then to Lenox, Massachusetts. And there was the transition, mostly psychological, of their having to face the reality that their attempts to keep one foot in Europe and another in America would not be possible.

But no matter where on the map the Bondys landed, they always seemed to become associated with prominent people. For example, a list of the school's sponsors, appearing in an undated catalogue (probably from 1941), included Dr. Thomas Mann (Princeton, New Jersey), the Nobel Prize–winning novelist; Dr. Karen Horney, the renowned German psychoanalyst; Dorothy Thompson Lewis (Barnard, Vermont), journalist and radio broadcaster known as the "First Lady of American Journalism"; and Mr. and Mrs. Winston Churchill (Cornish, New Hampshire). No relation to Sir

Winston, this Churchill (1871–1947) was one of the bestselling American novelists of the early twentieth century and lived three miles from Windsor.[72]

Windsor Mountain Moves to Manchester, Vermont

After leaving Juniper Hill Farm in Windsor in the spring of 1940, the Bondys reopened their school in Manchester in the fall of that same year. In larger quarters, there were now fourteen students, ages eight to seventeen. Nine of them were Americans, and five were from other countries. The school would stay there for four years (1940–44).

In Manchester, too, the Bondys touched celebrity, albeit indirectly, when they leased another beautiful manse with a significant past. A flyer, prepared by the current owner, contains the story of the property's origins:

> *Albert Gilbert, a Chicago railroad industrialist, and his friend Robert Todd Lincoln, President Lincoln's son, created two vast neighboring estates in Manchester. (Lincoln's estate, Hildene, is now a historic site and popular tourist destination). When Gilbert died in 1906, his banker, James Wilbur, purchased the estate and named it Wilburton Hall. After his death in 1928, the family's fortune plummeted with the Wall Street Crash [and] the entire property, except for the hill and the mansion, was sold. During World War II, the Wilbur family leased the mansion to the Windsor Mountain School, a school for the children of Berlin's artists and high society who had fled from Nazi Germany.*

After Windsor Mountain left Manchester, Wilburton Hall became the Wilburton Inn (1945). Purchased in 1987 by Dr. Albert Levis and his wife, Georgette (now deceased), the inn is a member of the Historic Hotels of America.

Two of the students on Windsor's Manchester campus who, according to the *Eighth Bulletin* (1943), received diplomas were Ann Mackinnon (1925–2009) and Winnetou Zuckmayer (1925–). Mackinnon wrote about Windsor Mountain in her memoirs and her 1944 diary, excerpts of which are contained in the biography of award-winning American poet Robert Creeley (1926–2005), to whom she was married for nearly ten years (1946–55).[73] Creeley's biographer describes Mackinnon as "a troubled, insecure

The Wilburton Inn in Manchester, Vermont, Windsor Mountain's second location in the United States. *Author's collection.*

loner, yet full of spunk"[74] and includes details related to the following: her evolving relationship with Creeley, her time at Windsor Mountain, taking Creeley to meet the Bondys, getting pregnant, being abandoned by Creeley and then going back to Windsor for respite.

Mackinnon was an orphan whose guardian decided that Ann, unhappy at school in Wellesley, Massachusetts, might prefer Windsor Mountain School. Since "Freud and psychoanalysis were all the rage," wrote Mackinnon, "Connie [her guardian] found the perfect solution—a school run by an authentic female Austrian psychiatrist, a former pupil of Freud's, who could be counted on to deal with any behaviors I might come up with for no more cost than a normal boarding school fee."[75]

Ann's guardian first sent her to Max and Gertrud's summer camp, where, upon her arrival, "the two Bondys came to look me over. Mrs. Bondy had snapping eyes and a determined smile, but aside from formalities, she only wanted to know if I had had my appendix out yet, and seemed disappointed at the answer" (her answer being that she had not). Mackinnon goes on:

Winthrop Estate, Lenox, Sold For Use as Private School

Groton Place, Long Owned by Late Grenville L. Winthrop, Bought for Windsor Mountain School for $50,000

(From Monday's Eagle)

LENOX — In the biggest residential real estate transaction in the Berkshires in some time Groton Place, the estate of the late Grenville L. Winthrop, was sold today to Dr. Max Bondy, head of the Windsor Mountain School of Manchester, Vt. The co-educational preparatory school will be transferred to its new home Sept. 1 although Dr. Bondy will take possession Aug. 1. The estate, valued at more than $150,-000, has been offered for sale for $90,000. Wheeler & Taylor Inc., of Great Barrington, who made the sale, announced no price but it is understood to be about $50,000.

With the announcement of the sale it was said that the school will not be incorporated in Massachusetts at present so Lenox will not lose any of the taxation on the porperty. The annual tax bill for Groton Place has been in the neighborhood of $5800. The aggregate value according to the assessors' books is $173,250, $85,000 for the mansion, $77,500 for the land and $10,750 for other property.

Long Established School

The Windsor Mountain School was operated for 20 years in pre-Nazi Germany and in Switzerland. It was moved to this country in 1939. There are 46 students enrolled for the fall season at a tuition of $1500 a year.

Both elementary and high school courses are offered with special opportunities in languages. Besides a well balanced curriculum, Windsor Mountain School offers students the usual sports, baseball, football, track, soccer, basketball and volleyball.

Mrs. Bondy, wife of the headmaster, who has an M.D. degree, looks after the health of the students.

Included in the enrollment are 10 English students. It is understood Dr. Bondy plans after the war to prepare for an exchange of students with the former school he operated in Switzerland, wherein some pupils will have opportunity for foreign study annually. Dr. Bondy will arrive shortly to prepare the school for the opening.

A headline in the *Berkshire Eagle*, July 17, 1944. *Courtesy of the Berkshire Eagle, Pittsfield, MA.*

Bondy was a tall man, mostly bald, with a sensitive, spiritual face. He sat on the edge of a straight chair in embarrassed silence like a farmer who had strayed into a lingerie shop. It turned out that neither one of them could speak English well enough to understand more than the simplest statements…Since it was a German school, we had breakfast, lunch, tea, dinner and a before-bed snack. With so much food, we were all in a state of energized excitement.[76]

In her diary, Ann also refers to her Latin classmate at Windsor Mountain Hugo Moser (1924–2007), a refugee from Nazi Germany, whom she described as "absolutely brilliant."[77] And apparently, he was, as he became an internationally recognized research scientist known for his work on Lorenzo's oil, the treatment named for Lorenzo Odone, a boy afflicted with ALD, an inherited metabolic disorder. Moser gained further fame when a movie, *Lorenzo's Oil*, brought to light the story of this complicated medical saga.[78]

After graduating from Windsor Mountain, Mackinnon returned to work as a counselor at the Bondys' camp. She then briefly attended Radcliffe but left for mental health reasons and studied at Berkshire Community College in Pittsfield, Massachusetts, not far from Lenox, before going on to Mount Holyoke, from which she graduated. Mackinnon continued to visit the Bondys after they moved the school from Manchester to the Berkshires.

Graduating from Windsor the same year as Ann Mackinnon was Winnetou Zuckmayer, whose father, Carl, was another member of German "high society" who, like Moser, had fled from Nazi Germany. Like the Bondys, he and his family had been among the refugees whom Dorothy Thompson, with input from President Roosevelt, had helped to come to America and then Vermont.

In 2012, Georgette Levis recalled that Winnetou, then around eighty, came to visit the Wilburton Inn, the site of her old school, in 2007 or 2008 and told Georgette that an only child of German refugees had drowned in the pond behind the main building while ice-skating. This story was confirmed by Mark Abramowicz, now a pediatrician, who has the distinction of being one of the few students who attended Windsor Mountain School both in Manchester and Lenox, after the Bondys purchased the Winthrop estate.

WINDSOR MOUNTAIN SCHOOL MOVES TO THE WINTHROP ESTATE IN LENOX, MASSACHUSETTS

After outgrowing their Manchester location, Max and Gertrud found a larger campus in the Berkshires, in Lenox, Massachusetts, another New England town. Like Windsor and Manchester, Lenox was compatible with the Bondy philosophy because it, too, was governed by the tradition of one man, one vote—the same system the Bondys had put into place at their school. Lenox also shared with the Vermont towns a rich and long history, unspoiled scenery, historic homes, cultural landmarks, museums, inns and restaurants and diverse opportunities for outdoor recreation. The Bondys understood that the setting of their school would be a selling point, and they would mention it when advertising the school.

While Windsor at last had "its own home," made possible with "the help of American friends," the Bondys expressed regret at having to leave Vermont, where, they said, they "had tried for a year in vain to find a place large enough for our school." In their report in the *Ninth Bulletin* of November 1944, the Bondys announced their move to Lenox and included the school's growth in numbers from 1939 to 1944 that had warranted their search for a bigger campus. Having started with three students in 1939, there were fifty-two by 1944.

The July 17, 1944 *Berkshire Eagle* article "Winthrop Estate Lenox, Sold for Use as Private School" noted that Groton Place, the estate of the late Grenville L. Winthrop, was sold to Dr. Max Bondy for about $50,000. Tuition at the school, according to the article, would be $1,500 a year. In a brochure—in which the Wheeler & Taylor real estate company had advertised the property for $90,000—the following description appeared:

> [It is a] *handsome home less than a mile from the center of town* [and] *Tanglewood, where the Berkshire Symphonic Festival is held...*[There are approximately] *ninety-five acres, native trees and shrubbery, and the views are magnificent.* [On the second floor] *are eleven bedrooms, on the third floor seven master bedrooms,* [and there is] *a Superintendent's cottage* [with] *ten rooms.* [There is also] *a studio building, poultry house, aquarium and bird home...*

C.S. Hayward, in his article "Public to Get First View of Groton Place," in the *Springfield Sunday Union and Republican* of August 15, 1943, noted that the property had also been graced with "brilliantly plumaged pheasants and proud peacocks stalking and strutting through the glades."

Grenville Lindall Winthrop (1864–1943), a descendant of John Winthrop (1588–1649), the founder and first governor of the Massachusetts Bay Colony, graduated from Harvard University (1886) and Harvard Law School (1889) but was not interested in law or banking, the family occupations. Instead, he made Lenox and Groton Place—named for the sixteenth-century English manor of his ancestors—his principal residence for forty-one years. With the expertise of the architectural firm that

An undated photo of Grenville L. Winthrop in his garden at Groton Place, Lenox, Massachusetts. *Harvard University Arts Museums/Fogg Museum.*

Sculpture on the grounds of Windsor Mountain School, originally commissioned by Grenville L. Winthrop for Groton Place. *From 1968 Windsor catalogue.*

Opposite: The Windsor Classhouse, formerly the "chicken coop" for the Winthrop estate. *From 1958 Windsor catalogue.*

designed the New York Public Library, Winthrop turned the building into a sprawling mansion with one of the most stunning private landscapes in America. And the "lawns, woodlands, and fountains, made to his design, gained him awards from the Massachusetts Horticultural Society."[79] (Though the marble benches and stone statuary are now covered with moss and deteriorating, one can still sense their former beauty.)

The Bondys later transformed many of the buildings on the Winthrop estate, including the "chicken coop" inhabited by Winthrop's fowl, which became a two-story building used for classrooms (the Classhouse), and his charming marble teahouse, which was later used by Windsor students as a newspaper office and, at times, a snack bar.

The Bondys had acquired an adjoining estate, Beaupre, and used its main building for a boys' dorm. "Students burned it down prior to Christmas break one year, and in its place an A-frame home used for faculty housing was built," said Mike Cunningham, current caretaker of the property. "And the buildings used for Winthrop's draft horses and his carriage barn were turned into dorms." Heinz Bondy added on to the art studio built for one of Grenville's daughters and made a home there for his family, noted Cunningham, who also said that Heinz gave Franny and Jim Hall a piece of the property on Hawthorne Street on which to build a house behind the

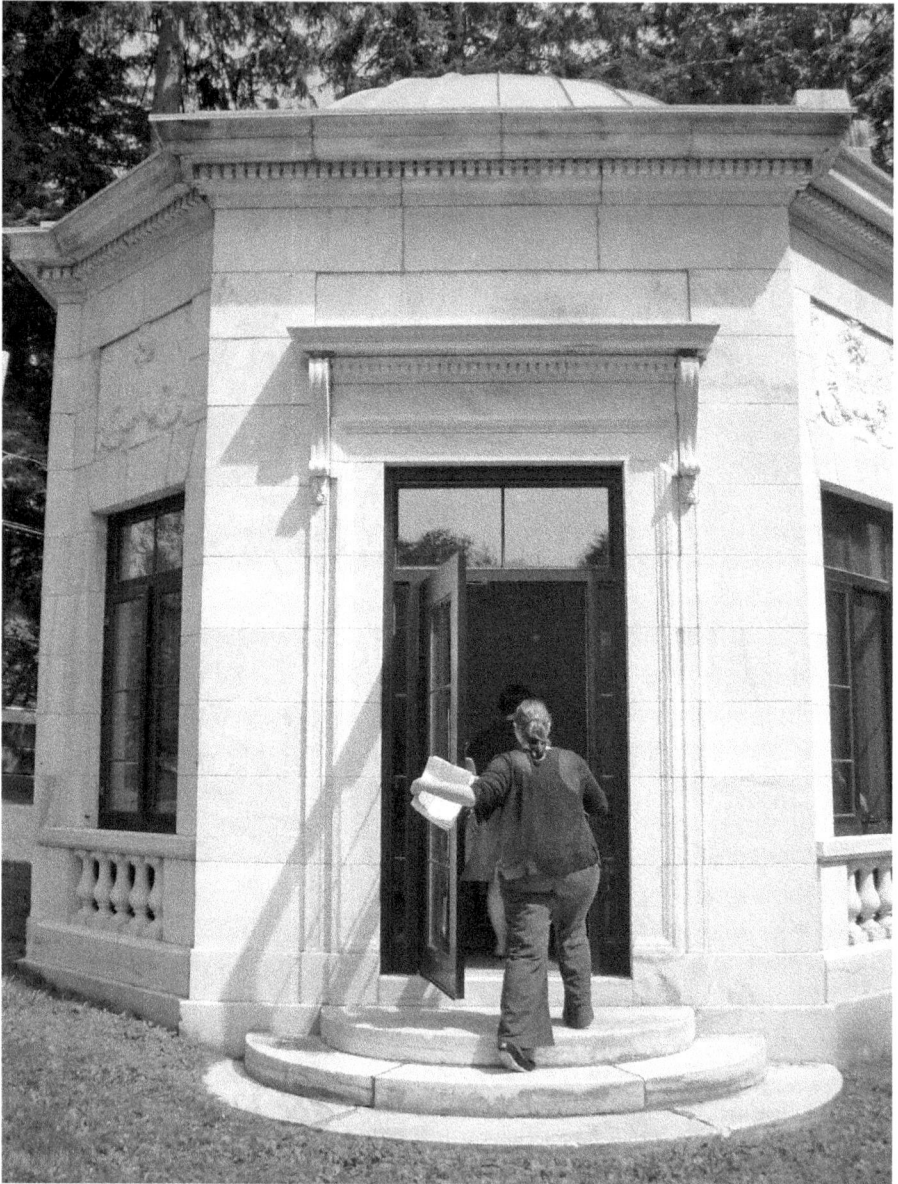

The marble teahouse built for Groton Place and used by Windsor students for a variety of purposes. *Author's collection.*

science building. "We just had to cross the lawn to get to the school," said Hall, whose two sons, Parnee and Terry, both attended Windsor Mountain. There are, Mike said, entrances to the property from 60 Hawthorne Street and 45 West Street.

WINTHROP'S GENEROSITY DOES NOT PROTECT HIM FROM SCANDAL

Grenville Winthrop, who served as president of the Lenox Library Association until the end of his life, was responsible for restoring and converting the former Colonial Courthouse on Main Street into the present, architecturally impressive Lenox Library, an achievement for which it seems apt to call him the "Father of the Lenox Library." Grenville's passion for art led to an "unparalleled collection of some four thousand works," including paintings by Renoir and van Gogh. He gave those works, along with one of the most important collections of Chinese art in the West, to Harvard University's Fogg Museum, a gift considered to be "the most important such bequest ever to an American university."[80]

But the generosity of this shy, reticent gentleman did not protect him from the scandal brought on by his two daughters. It was said that Winthrop had decided to buy his West Street estate to be near his mother, Kate, a friend of author Edith Wharton's (who lived nearby at the Mount) and with whom she would gossip and drink tea in New York and share talks in the Lenox Library.[81] Grenville hoped that his mother (whose Lenox home, Ethelwynde, was located on Yokun Street) could help keep an eye on his two daughters. Winthrop kept them in strict seclusion because, allegedly, he wanted to prevent them from ever marrying, lest they meet the same fate as their mother, who became an invalid and mentally unstable after the birth of their first daughter and later died in childbirth with the second.[82]

But Grenville and his mother were unsuccessful in their efforts to keep the girls from creating what turned out to be a huge scandal among their aristocratic crowd. "Winthrop Sisters in Dual Elopement, Daughters of Wealthy New York and Lenox Man Wed Chauffeur and Electrician" was the headline that appeared in the *New York Times* of September 7, 1924, and in every other major newspaper in the country. Miss Emily, thirty-one, a sculptress, married her father's chauffeur, Corey Lucien Miles, and Miss

Kate, twenty-four, married a young electrician and caretaker of her father's chicken house, Darwin Spurr Morse. The papers added, "Mr. Winthrop was said to be shocked and grieved..."[83]

While there is much more to this saga, including Winthrop's estrangement from both daughters, suffice it to say that both young women were nonconformists in their day and had challenged the status quo. Unbeknownst to them, however, they had set the stage for the nonconformists who would come to Groton Place/Windsor Mountain School some twenty years later.

ALUMNI IN THEIR OWN WORDS: DR. MARK ABRAMOWICZ, PEDIATRICIAN

Mark Abramowicz was one of the few students who began attending Windsor Mountain (early 1944) in Manchester and then briefly attended the school after it moved to the Berkshires. His was a family of refugees from Vienna who, he said, "fled soon after the Anschluss [Germany's annexation of Austria in 1938]." They risked their lives escaping to France before finally arriving in America with the help of Princess Maria Bonaparte, a psychologist and friend of Freud's. Said Abramowicz:

> In December '43, just as my father was reestablishing himself as a doctor in New York City [having practiced at first in rural New York state], he was killed in a bizarre accident. My mother and I moved to Boston so she could study to become a social worker. She needed a place for me, so I went to Windsor Mountain, from January 1944 to June '44, entering the seventh grade. I remember getting off the train by myself in Manchester with my valise; it was scary. Then I attended the Bondys' summer camp, where I and a few others caught polio, perhaps in the swimming pool, as the disease was contagious and the pool may not have had chlorine. [He ultimately survived without any paralysis.] I had to skip a semester [Fall 1945] when I was hospitalized in Troy, New York. I recuperated in Boston and then returned to Windsor Mountain in Lenox for a semester [January '45 to June]. I went to the camp again and then to public school in Boston.
>
> Many of the students were displaced persons from all over, and there were locals as well. And [there was] a kid who went around saying his

Max Bondy with
Barbara Kronick
(Greenfeld), age twelve,
at Windsor Mountain
School, 1949. *Courtesy of
Barbara Greenfeld.*

*father was in jail for rape or murder. There were small classes, mixed ages
in the same class and sports on an informal basis—basketball, some hiking
and skiing...*

*Gertrud was charming, attractive and responsive. One example of that
was when some kid put toothpaste on a kid's penis, and she called them
in about it. And she was always twirling her hair at the assemblies. Max
was an authority figure, kind of scary to a little boy, severe, always red in
the face. If he ever smiled, I never saw it. At the evening assembly every
night, Max did all the talking...Two recent immigrants, Adolf Busch,
violinist, and Rudy Serkin, pianist, who my mother once met in Vienna
gave a concert at the school, playing duets.*

There might have been other students who, like Abramowicz, attended Windsor at two of its locations, but he is likely the only one to have visited the Lenox campus many years later, when his own daughter was a violin student one summer at the Boston University Tanglewood Institute, which took over the former Windsor campus in 1980. Said Abramowicz, "When I visited her there, it was like coming full circle."

Like Abramowicz, Barbara Kronick Greenfeld, '49–50, was a child of refugees. But her Ukrainian immigrant parents were forced to give her up for adoption, and she lived at the Boston Home for Jewish Children, which in 1949 sent her to Windsor Mountain School, where she was enrolled in the seventh grade. Barbara had already gone to live with the Kronicks, a lawyer and a teacher, in North Adams, Massachusetts, and they would eventually formally adopt her. Though only there for a year, memories of Windsor are etched into Barbara's brain, and she recalls many things with emotion: her picture being taken with Max, talking with Gertrud ("Grandma"), walking into Lenox on Wednesdays to sit at the soda fountain at Hagyard's Drug Store and on Saturdays going to the Little Cinema in the Berkshire Museum in Pittsfield, where she saw Laurence Olivier in *King Henry V*. But Barbara said she especially cherished the times with her teacher, Lydia Bills, under the tree in front of the manse, where she learned to love Shakespeare.

ALUMNI IN THEIR OWN WORDS: T.R. JACKSON

Unlike refugee Mark Abramowicz, T.R. Jackson came from a Protestant family with a long history in America and entered Windsor Mountain School in Lenox in the fall of 1945. Said Jackson:

My mother was a coal miner's daughter who ended up going to Radcliffe. My father's father had been chief chemist at DuPont and was from a fancy line of Boston folks. My father went to fight in World War I and then graduated from MIT. The Depression turned him into a socialist, and he spent the rest of his life traveling from one cooperative community [commune] to another looking for nirvana. My sister, Alice, preceded me at Windsor. By word of mouth, my mother had heard about the school.

T.R. Jackson (pictured here at age seventeen), Windsor Mountain student from 1945 to 1948. *Courtesy of T.R. Jackson.*

Somebody said to her, "You have a troubled daughter, and there's this place where there's a psychoanalyst."

I attended Windsor from 1945 to 1948 but never graduated. I went on to Black Mountain College for three years and likewise never completed my degree. After Black Mountain, I ended up in the electronics field, where my designing skills were used by various entrepreneurs. One of my creations were devices that are part of the system that monitors large printing presses and can count everything that goes into and out of the press. They are now all over the world. I'm proud of that and of staying free of religion.

The Bondys were an overwhelming presence. The place was infused with Germanism—everyone talking German. I was less impressed with the academics—there was no physics teacher there [there was later], *and that was my passion—but I gained much that is still with me, thanks to the European faculty and the diversity of the place. I remember several students were displaced persons, some with numbers on their arms. At the time, I was not aware that the Bondys were Jewish, but everyone knew their story of escape from the Nazis. But I thought it was because of their philosophy.*

Every evening after dinner, Max would expound on the news of the world, its dangers, and that was powerful and remained with me. My notion of Max was one of being somewhat childlike. For example, Max was in love with his Oldsmobile 88; his infatuation with this car was so strange. [Annemarie had noted that Max's father was one of the first people in Germany to own a car, and both men were "passionate about automobiles."] *Max was never able to completely become "American." He, more than Gertrud, seemed to need to continue the attachment to the past.*

I was struck by the obliviousness of the Bondys. They appeared to me not to believe in the legitimacy of authority and delegated tremendous authority to teachers. Students would be organized into groups under a teacher [similar to what Max had experienced in the German Youth Movement], *who was cleared to do whatever he wanted.* [T.R. related the following story to illustrate the downside of that arrangement]*:*

I was under the authority of a teacher, B.C., and he had even more power because he was one of the few who had a car. Normally we were allowed to go to Lenox on Wednesdays and to Pittsfield on Saturdays. But if you were with a teacher, you could do anything and go anywhere anytime. You could even smoke in your rooms. So this teacher, and maybe others, was free to indulge in child abuse. I was one of the victims. I don't know if I can say I have been affected by that abuse, but the guy was a scumbag. This stuff was never talked about, but much of that kind of thing went on undiscovered. I never said anything about this experience at the time because the Bondys might have hurt _____ [referring to a female teacher he treasured and with whom he had "a hot romance," something for which she would have been fired and he thrown out of school]. *But only three of us knew about it. I'm not going to be a judge when it comes to that kind of thing today, though I might have a dimmer view if it was a male teacher and female student.*

CONNECTIONS: BLACK MOUNTAIN COLLEGE AND WINDSOR MOUNTAIN SCHOOL

Students graduating from Windsor in the 1940s went on to schools like Harvard, Radcliffe, Bard, Columbia, MIT, Cornell and Bennington. But there was an especially close connection between Windsor Mountain and

Left: Jim Hall, literature and English teacher at Windsor Mountain School. *From 1969 Windsor yearbook.*

Below: Windsor students involved in an outdoor work project. *From 1970 Windsor yearbook.*

Black Mountain College (1933–57), in Asheville, North Carolina. Both schools were short-lived and closed by bankruptcy but had very vibrant lives. Operating along the lines of John Dewey's principles, both were experimental and interdisciplinary and emphasized the arts. Faculty and students came from all over the world and included refugees from Nazi Germany.

According to Franny Hall, when she and Jim went to teach at Windsor in 1947, Jim, who had studied at Black Mountain (though he received his BA from UCLA and his MA from the University of Wisconsin), brought with him new ideas from the college, like student work programs, which he then organized and led at Windsor.

Jim told the Bondys that "there might be others from the college who would be good for the school," and soon after that, "three people from Black Mountain came to teach at Windsor," said Hall. They, in turn, inspired many Windsor students to go on to the college. Among them were T.R. and his two sisters, Lucy and Alice; Peter Heinemann, '46–48, (1931–2010), who became one of the finest post–World War II figurative painters in America; Donald "Duck" Daley, who returned to Windsor to teach for several years; and poet and potter Cynthia Homire, '49, a 1954 graduate, friend of T.R.'s[84] and part of the cadre of artists who live and work in Taos, New Mexico. During an interview related to an exhibition of her work at the Black Mountain College Museum and Arts Center in 2014, Homire told a reporter that while studying at the college, she had "rubbed shoulders with the pantheon, a few bellies, too…jitterbugged with Rauschenberg…[and] shared steak with William Carlos Williams."[85]

1948 POSTWAR SUMMER ABROAD

On June 29, 1948, Max and Gertrud traveled to Europe with eighteen students to study and tour, and Franny and Jim Hall (with three-year-old son, Parnee, in tow) went along to tutor and chaperone. "We sailed on the SS *Marine Tiger*," said Franny, "and spent most of the time in a rented hotel in the Alps of Switzerland." (According to a July 3, 1947 article in the *Berkshire Eagle* titled "Head of Windsor Mt. School to Establish College Abroad," the Bondys had also gone to Switzerland the year before to found a junior college in Engelberg. They explained in a four-page brochure dated January 1946 that its purpose would be to bring American and European students together "to destroy Hitlerism as a philosophy and replace it with higher ideals." The closest they came to fulfilling this plan was this trip to Europe with students in 1948.)

Said Franny:

> *At the end of the summer, Max rented a bus that went over the Alps and down to Rome and Venice for two weeks. It was so beautiful. One of the students said when we got to Rome, "I have to meet the pope." Gertrud sent me as the only Catholic, though lapsed, along with the student. So we went to this hall in the Vatican, and a cardinal accompanied the Pope, who walked along the line of people and greeted them. And when he extended his hand to us, we knelt and kissed his ring.*

(The pope asked Hall if her student was a good girl, and Hall said she told the pope sarcastically, "Oh, no, she's very bad!")

In the rough draft of a press release about that summer in Switzerland, shared by Marcia Ruff, historian, Max is asked about his plans for the next summer and whether there would be another trip: "Dr. Bondy smiled uncertainly, 'It depends upon the foreign situation.'" At that time, the Cold War was heating up. They did not return the next summer.

Windsor's last graduation of the decade took place on June 4, 1949, and was a two-day affair. On Saturday, at 7:30 a.m., there was a performance of music and three plays, followed by a buffet supper. And the next day, Sunday, June 5, seventeen students received their diplomas. Dr. Curt Bondy delivered the commencement address, which was followed by dinner at 1:00 p.m.

Chapter 4

What Was Unique about the Education at Windsor Mountain School?: A Handbook for Humanistic Education, or Why Windsor Still Matters

Humanism means respect for the human being, regardless of age, sex, creed or race. It means a sense of empathy, the ability to identify with others. Humanism portrays a kind of open communication, a tolerant sharing with others. Humanism is a philosophy which believes in man's capacity to improve human relations [through] justice instead of power. Humanism values reason. Most of all, humanism is for freedom of inquiry, for values, for ethics, for moral standards.
—George Roeper, remarks from "Senior Dinner Speech," June 6, 1981, at The Roeper School

WHY WINDSOR MOUNTAIN SCHOOL STILL MATTERS

Windsor's curriculum consisted of courses typical of a college preparatory school. Students did homework, took tests, wrote papers, prepared projects, took the SATs and did what they needed to do to get into college, though that was not everyone's goal. For example, Nate Steele, '72, who went on to become an outdoor educator, said he never took a standardized test. Students could make such choices. Yet Windsor Mountain consistently met the

Study hall in the library of the main manse at Windsor Mountain. *From a late 1960s Windsor catalogue.*

requirements necessary for accreditation by the New England Association of Schools and Colleges.

However, when former students were asked about the education they received at Windsor Mountain, there was less talk about the academics and more about the "atmosphere of the school," which was, they said, permeated by values like tolerance and trust and where, one student said, "If we went off the deep end, we knew we would be brought back to safety." According to Dave Bellar, '68, it was an atmosphere that, in a majority of cases, met the unique needs of Windsor students, some of whom he described as "square pegs who couldn't fit into the round holes of public schools."

Today, American schools, burdened by excessive standardized testing, are still geared primarily to "round holes"—that is, the homogenization of education that deprives children of individual attention. According to several current news articles, parents have been speaking out against

Cover of the 1954 Windsor yearbook. *Courtesy of Martha Peskin.*

such testing, which they say is dehumanizing and dominating education at the expense of children's learning. They are arguing that values such as compassion, curiosity, creativity and critical thinking are not being taught because they can't be measured on a standardized test.[86] Betsy Ryan, a former student who said she was inspired to go into teaching because of her experience at Windsor, believes that Windsor Mountain's model of humanistic education can "show public schools what they CAN be without the data-driven instruction heralded as the way to improve instruction." The values that she encountered at Windsor Mountain constitute a handbook on humanistic education and help to explain why Windsor Mountain School still matters.

The Bondys did not simply convey through speeches and writing the values that comprised their humanistic philosophy. They also put into place tangible structures and steps by which students could learn these values and practice them.

Individualizing Instruction

Windsor Mountain provided an atmosphere, students said, in which they were free to explore their personal interests. Nate Steele, for example, said, "If you wanted to learn something, Windsor would find someone to teach it. Some of us wanted to learn about cars, and they arranged for Steve Futterman to come in and teach auto mechanics and electronics."

Catya von Karolyi, '72, spoke of her English course with Cherie Huntress, in which she "was allowed to do an independent project, to design a utopian school—after I'd read all the literature I could get my hands on. Cherie allowed me to work with her to individualize my educational experience—something that teachers at Windsor would often do but that didn't happen in most places in those days." That was true also of collaboration among Windsor faculty members, who offered interdisciplinary courses like "The 20th Century," in which English teachers Franny and Jim Hall and "Duck" Daley, a history teacher, integrated content from both areas.

School Setting

In discussing what was unique about their education, alumni also talked about the setting of the school—the "look of the place" and the beauty of Windsor's natural surroundings. They recalled the expansive lawns,

Students sledding on a hill near the main manse at Windsor Mountain. *From 1971 Windsor yearbook.*

Teacher Haldor Reinholt holding class on the lawn. *From 1969 Windsor yearbook.*

Students working in the Windsor biology classroom. *From 1958 Windsor yearbook.*

the foliage around the gorgeous stone mansion and, off in the distance, the rolling Berkshire Hills. Von Karolyi, whose father taught at the school, wrote, "It was pretty magical growing up where there were those estate gardens and marble fountains, pools, balustrades and sculptures. The thyme-covered hills were amazing places to roll down in summer or sled in winter."

In his memoir, John Gialuco, '66, described walking the "stunning, beautiful grounds," the "tree-soaked massive front lawn" and the "handmade marble and granite back patio."[87] It was a privilege to learn amidst such exquisite beauty, alumni said, and many remembered how several of the faculty members, including Haldor Reinholt and Bob Sagor, would hold classes out on the lawn as often as possible because of the aesthetics of the environment. In fact, the Bondys were ahead of their time in conveying the importance of preserving that beauty long before the arrival of the environmental movement.

Beyond the campus, too, students experienced natural beauty. For example, said Jonathan Shapiro, '66, now a psychologist, "Every year there was a three- to four-hour morning hike up Mount Greylock led by Rex Reckendorf, and we'd get to watch the sun rise and then eat breakfast at the summit."

TRUSTING RELATIONSHIPS BETWEEN TEACHERS AND STUDENTS

Having the chance to learn *with* their teachers both in and outside the classroom and getting to know them on a first-name basis made a difference in their lives, said many alumni. Jon Shapiro spoke about playing his drums out on the lawn with music teacher Sushil Mukherjee, who played several Indian instruments.

Students could observe teachers, many of them artists in their own right, including weaver Edith Reckendorf. They could also listen to English teacher, author and poet Gerry Hausman reciting his poetry or to

Edith Reckendorf, weaver and art teacher at Windsor Mountain, at her loom. *From 1967 Windsor yearbook.*

Windsor Mountain
language teacher Quentin
"Label" LaBelle. *From 1967
Windsor yearbook.*

music teacher Harry Rubenstein, who played classical music on the piano every morning before breakfast. Trusting relationships were also formed on the soccer field, at "the jam sessions with teachers Sid Hausman and John Huntress" or while sitting at dinner with a faculty member. Linda Fields, '63, recalled, "If you sat at the same table as [language teacher] Quentin 'Label' LaBelle on a night when he didn't like what was on the menu, he would take the whole table to Friendly's in Lee for dinner."

DEMOCRACY: FREEDOM WITH RESPONSIBILITY

Students learned about democracy by practicing it. For example, Windsor's Student Council and Student Court, endowed with extensive powers, made all nonacademic rules and could even expel peers for serious infractions. Heinz Bondy, along with a faculty member elected by the students, attended the meetings and acted as mentors while student leaders deliberated and debated. Heinz, however, was reluctant, said several alumni, to expel students because he believed—or hoped—that, given freedom, students would become responsible and self-disciplined. John Gialuco said he appreciated that philosophy and "sensed a feeling of freedom" when he came to Windsor. This was after having experienced earlier what he called "the repressive, dogmatic educational prison system, where I was running out of tricks to survive."

Every night of the week, assemblies were held in the theater, where Bondy would make announcements and share important news and students could freely express their concerns. Charlie Parriott, '68, now an acclaimed glass artist, said, "Those assemblies gave me the confidence to speak truth to power and, later in life, to say what I think." Such opportunities for free expression helped many students discover leadership skills they never knew they had. Peter Whitehead, for example, who came to Windsor after being suspended from a couple other schools for "being a nonconformist," said, "Here I finally fit in! In a month, I was up for school president; it was transforming. I kept pricking myself that I had found this place."

THE ARTS: CENTRAL TO HUMANISTIC EDUCATION

The Bondys viewed the arts not only as aesthetic education but also as a means of empowering young people. Art enabled students to discover themselves and their creative powers while also giving them a means of making a personal statement. Practically every art and craft was offered: sculpture, painting, drawing, weaving, sewing, leatherwork, metal and woodwork, ceramics and photography, as well as theater, poetry, creative writing, music and dance. There was a madrigal group and instrumental instruction, as well as frequent field trips to museums, theaters and concerts. Franny Hall put on several plays a year that Windsor students performed not only on campus but also at other venues, such as Lenox High School. And events like Parents' Weekend, held along with the annual May Fair celebration, a fundraiser for the school, gave students the opportunity to exhibit their artistic talents, a culmination of all of their artistic endeavors for that year. As humanists, the Bondys believed students could—and should—make their world more

Student Marty Kaufman in the pottery studio at Windsor Mountain. *From 1968 Windsor yearbook.*

beautiful. So the arts were on more than an equal footing with the rest of the curriculum at Windsor Mountain, which might be why so many alumni went on to become artists, actors and musicians.

A "FRIENDLY" SCHOOL AND COMMUNITY: EDUCATION FOR COOPERATION

Max Bondy preferred the term "friendly school" to the term "progressive school" because, for Max, a friendly school was the key to the kind of emotional training that would reduce fears and violent impulses. A friendly school was one that provided a caring community—a refuge where you could be who you were without fear of ridicule or prejudice and where there was no need for defensiveness. A sense of community, Bondy believed, would also inspire students to work together to do good both within and beyond the campus. The message was "cooperation is better than competition," and they worked together in the classroom, on the field or court, outdoors on work projects, on stage or behind the stage or in organizing events like the May Fair. On the other hand, considering the awards that Windsor's sports teams earned, they could be extremely competitive when necessary.

MIND/BODY BALANCE

The Bondys believed in balancing academics with physical activity, a tradition that Max Bondy carried with him from his days as part of the German Youth Movement and his association with educators like Kurt Hahn and others in the German Country Boarding School Movement. For these pioneers in outdoor recreation, a healthy body meant a healthy mind. For athletes, there were teams in at least six different sports, and for the general student body, choices from hiking and calisthenics to square-dancing.

Students making a human pyramid on the lawn near the manse. *From 1969 Windsor yearbook.*

A SOCIAL CONSCIENCE

Because the Bondys believed that students should stand up for justice against oppression of all kinds, teachers frequently took busloads of students to antiwar marches, civil rights demonstrations and anti-nuclear rallies, among others. Students remembered going down to Washington, D.C., in 1967 during the Vietnam War era to participate in the March on the Pentagon and, in 1969, to the October Moratorium March against the war. And when, for example, twenty-seven men in the military were court-martialed for antiwar activity and given prison sentences at the San Francisco Presidio stockade in 1968, students went to Pittsfield and carried posters calling for the release of the "Presidio 27," as they were called.

Windsor students marching in Pittsfield, Massachusetts, on behalf of the Presidio 27, soldiers arrested for protesting against the Vietnam War. *From 1969 Windsor yearbook.*

NOT JUST TOLERANCE, BUT LOVE

Individual differences were not only accepted; they were supported. Teacher Bob Blafield and others said that Heinz was at his most decisive when he saw someone treat a student unjustly because of his or her differences. He wouldn't tolerate that kind of thing. And Gertrud, in her "sessions," offered students unconditional love. She and Max spoke often about how love was the path to making a better world, which they devoted themselves to accomplishing through education. Martha Peskin recalled that there were students who found that love by gathering around Gertrud; others hung out with Heinz. Some found personal connections with faculty or with one another, though, sadly, and for reasons they couldn't say, several students admitted that "some lost souls never found the peace and love they searched for."

DIVERSITY AND AN INTERNATIONAL, MULTIRACIAL FACULTY

From the beginning of their mission as educators, the Bondys were fierce believers in diversity and equal rights. Schule Marienau was one of the first co-educational, multicultural boarding schools in Germany, and Windsor Mountain was the first in Berkshire County. Students came from many nations and from every race, religion and class—and likewise, there was an international faculty.

Initially, Max and Gertrud brought to the school European scholars they had known in Germany, many of whom, like themselves, were refugees, including the Reckendorfs, who had taught at Schule Marienau (Otto "Rex" in the sciences and Edith in the art of weaving). Math and physics teachers Klara and Dr. Kornel Bernatsky had fled—like the six Hungarian students at Windsor—during the 1956 Hungarian uprising against the Soviet Union. Others included Karl Boecher, from Berlin, an art historian who taught Latin and German, and Dr. Oldrich Prochazka, a teacher of economics and social studies from Czechoslovakia, where he had been the country's first finance minister. Also from Czechoslovakia was Jan "Gerdi" Wiener, Gertrud's nephew, who taught European history, and his wife, Zuzana, who taught Russian. Mathematics teacher Haldor Reinholt was from Norway,

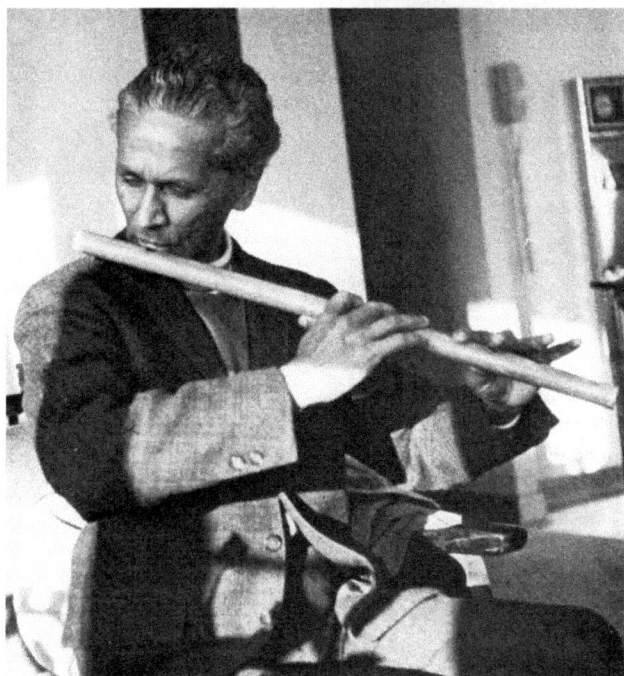

Top: Social sciences teacher Dr. Oldrich Prochazka. *From 1967 Windsor yearbook.*

Left: Sushil Mukherjee, artist, musician and Windsor teacher and director of humanities. *From 1970 Windsor yearbook.*

Top: David "Dave" Gunn, Windsor baseball, basketball and soccer coach and athletic director. *Courtesy of Wray Gunn.*

Left: Windsor basketball championship logo of 1969. *From 1969 Windsor yearbook.*

and Sushil Mukherjee (painter, writer and musician at Windsor); his wife, Gouri, a psychologist; and their son, Ronendra, '64, were from India. (Mukherjee's friend Ravi Shankar would sometimes visit, said John Gialuco, "and play the sitar while we ate dinner.") Milan Milicivec, from Serbia, was Windsor Mountain's head maintenance man who also taught carpentry, and his wife, "Mama Milan," was head housekeeper.

Several students also remembered the "dignity" of David "Dave" Gunn, whose African American roots in the Berkshires date back to the Revolutionary War. He coached baseball, basketball and soccer and, for a time, was athletic director, given the task of recruiting good players. Dave's son, Wray, said, "Dad produced the most powerful basketball teams in Windsor Mountain's history that defeated college freshman teams and other top-ranked schools in the area." Gunn set the precedent for Windsor's winning reputation, which continued under other outstanding coaches through the 1960s.

"Being exposed to such teachers was incredibly special," said Roselle Van Nostrand.

As Jeannie Whitehead looked through yearbook pictures of the faculty with me, she said, "Every one of these teachers is a story! How do you know where to stop?" Indeed, that decision wasn't easy, since most teachers were memorable for their excellence, albeit a few for less-than-admirable traits. One teacher, for example, was recalled for his aggressive behavior in class while under the influence. But in the end, alumni professed again and again that the lessons they learned from their mentors both inside and outside the classroom continue to impact their lives.

Chapter 5

The 1950s and Early '60s: Windsor as a Place of Refuge, Diversity and Utopian Possibilities

Herb Denton's father was a principal in Little Rock, Arkansas, and they had to get Herb away; they were afraid he'd be killed.
—Lesley Larsen Albert, '61, talking about Valedictorian Herbert Denton Jr., '61[88]

To a large extent, Windsor Mountain was an island. This was a time of racial turmoil, but at Windsor you couldn't tell the difference between races—all were equal. It was in the early '60s, when it was popular to have a few foreign students at prep schools. Diversity was considered important as an indirect way of teaching students about other cultures.
—Cadman Atta Mills, PhD, '63, ambassador to the United States from Ghana and former economic advisor to his brother, the late president of Ghana, John Atta Mills

On April 16, 1951, Max Bondy died in Boston at the age of fifty-eight. Gertrud continued as director, and their son, Heinz, took over as headmaster, remaining in that position until the school closed in 1975. Under Heinz's leadership, Windsor Mountain's reputation grew along with the number and diversity of its students.

Enrollment at Windsor Mountain in the fall of 1952 was a record 80 students (45 boys, 35 girls) and 15 faculty members. By February 1963, the numbers had more than doubled, with 205 students and 25 faculty members.[89] This remarkable growth might have been facilitated by ads the Bondys periodically placed in large urban newspapers, one of which Judy Kirsch Levin saved. The ad, which was taken from an undated *New York*

Times (but was possibly clipped by her family in 1954, when she was looking for the "right" school) reads:

WINDSOR MOUNTAIN SCHOOL: Co-educational college preparation in Berkshires. Grades 8–12. Daily counseling. Small classes. Friendly atmosphere. Music, art, dramatics, work projects, riding, skiing, all sports. Exc. College record. Dr. Gertrude Bondy, Box 508-A, Lenox, MA

A PLACE OF REFUGE AND DIVERSITY

A September 19, 1955 article in the *Berkshire Eagle* titled "Windsor Mt. School Opens with 118 Boys, Girls Enrolled" referenced Windsor's growing diversity:

Continuing a basic policy of mixing racial, religious and economic groups, the school is granting this year partial scholarships to 40 per cent of the student body...This was the first private school in this area to include Negro students and teachers. In 1946, the headmaster hired a Negro [music] teacher, Miss Anne DeRemus of New York City. This year's president of the student council is George Crockett, a Negro from Detroit.

Bill Dobbs shared the following story about George Crockett and his family:

The Crockett family was part of the long history of African Americans at Windsor Mountain School. The father's dissident politics surely had an impact on the entire family, and that may be why three siblings ended up at Windsor Mountain, years before Harry Belafonte and Sidney Poitier were Windsor parents. Elizabeth Crockett Hicks, '54; the Honorable George W. Crockett III, '56; and Dr. Ethelene Crockett Jones, '58, were from Detroit—and all three graduated from Windsor Mountain. Their parents were remarkable. George Crockett Jr. was a lawyer, judge and congressman and outspoken on civil rights, and their mother, Ethelene Crockett, was an obstetrician. Crockett Jr. helped to found the National Lawyers Guild and defended communists, for which he drew a term in federal prison for contempt of court. It was during the time that he had national notoriety that his kids were at Windsor Mountain.

The Crocketts weren't the only family, according to Dobbs, who sought refuge at Windsor Mountain for their offspring because of government harassment. Jo Wilkinson's, '64, father, Frank, an award-winning civil liberties activist, and his wife, Jean, were targets of McCarthyism. When he appeared before the House Un-American Activities Committee in 1956 and 1958, Wilkinson refused to answer questions about his party membership and was jailed for nine months in 1961 for contempt of Congress. His wife, Jean, was fired from her teaching position for refusing to cooperate with McCarthy-era investigations.[90] At one point, their house in Los Angeles was firebombed.

Adrienne Belafonte, the eldest daughter of actor-singer and activist Harry Belafonte, had as a roommate Lulah Durr, '67, when she arrived at Windsor as an eighth grader in 1962. "As I understand it," wrote Adrienne in a January 18, 2013 e-mail, "Lulah's house had been firebombed because her father was a [white] civil rights lawyer and she was sent east for safety reasons." Lulah's mother, Virginia Foster Durr (1903–1999), wrote in her autobiography:

> *By the time of the Regal Café case, living in Montgomery was like living in the midst of a storm. You never knew what was going to happen. We worried for the black people and for ourselves, but mostly for our children... Lulah was in Bellingrath School in Montgomery.* [Friends in the North] *got her a scholarship to the Windsor Mountain School. That support made a tremendous difference to us.*[91]

Both Clifford Durr (1899–1975) and Virginia are included in Peter Dreier's book *The 100 Greatest Americans of the 20ᵗʰ Century: A Social Justice Hall of Fame.*[92] A civil liberties activist during the McCarthy era, Durr left his position at the Federal Communications Commission (FCC) in 1948, when he knew he would be forced to administer loyalty oaths to all FCC employees, and the couple then moved to Montgomery, Alabama, where Durr had come from. Virginia, who was considered a "heroine [along with Rosa Parks] of the civil rights movement," had organized protests against the poll tax and lynching and was eventually subpoenaed to testify before the federal hearings organized in the mid-'50s by Senator Eastland to "uncover Communists."[93] She had secured a scholarship for Parks in 1955 to the progressive, interracial Highlander Folk School in Tennessee, where she received her political education; and it was only four months later that Parks refused to give up her seat on the bus, thus igniting the Montgomery bus boycott.

Maurice Eldridge, '57, in H.H. Milne's play *Mr. Pim Passes By*, directed by Franny Hall. *Courtesy of Franny Hall.*

There were other young women who also found a haven at Windsor Mountain School. For example, Judy Kirsch, a Jewish girl from a well-off family in Florida, was contending with difficult circumstances—albeit different from Durr's but no less challenging. Said Levin, "My father was a flight surgeon in the navy, and I went to nineteen different schools by the time I finished high school. Windsor sort of saved my life."

In 1954, Heinz went down to Washington, D.C., to recruit African American youth with academic potential. Maurice Eldridge, '57, a student in one of D.C.'s segregated schools at the time, remembered the day Heinz—and his Pontiac convertible—arrived at his school. After attending Windsor as a scholarship student, Eldridge went on to graduate from Swarthmore in '61 and then returned to Windsor to teach for two years (1965–67), becoming a protégé of Heinz's and essentially a member of the Bondy family. According to the *Berkshire Eagle*, he became one of the first black administrators at a private school when Heinz made him assistant headmaster, a position he held from 1967 to 1975. Following that experience, Eldridge held the position of principal at the Duke Ellington School of the Arts in D.C. (1979–89), after which he returned to Swarthmore, where he is now vice-president of college and community relations and executive assistant to the president. On caringbridge.com, Eldridge posted a testimonial to Heinz Bondy the day after he died (February 19, 2014), in which he said, "Windsor Mountain led me to a life focused on educating with the aim of doing for others and helping to make this a more just and humane world. In other words, I live the life Heinz modeled."

In his baccalaureate address, delivered at Swarthmore on May 30, 2009, and available online, Eldridge movingly takes the reader on his life's journey, during which he "crossed many borders" and felt the sting of racism. He spoke of coming to Windsor Mountain in 1954, the year that the Supreme Court, in its *Brown v. Board of Education* decision, made segregated schools unlawful.[94] Said Eldridge, "It was a homecoming for me—a rarity among New England prep schools in those days. Windsor was co-ed, multiracial [and] a haven, too, for European refugees, including my new friends, people who had survived concentration camps…All this visited upon the staid old New England town of Lenox."

Szmulek Rozental, who changed his name to Stephan Ross, was one of the concentration camp survivors whom Eldridge befriended. He was a "big, gangly, loveable kid who came to our house often," remembered Franny Hall. And for Ross, Windsor did, indeed, become a haven.

ALUMNI IN THEIR OWN WORDS: STEPHAN ROSS (SZMULEK ROZENTAL), '55

From the age of nine to fourteen, Szmulek Rozental was an inmate in ten different Nazi death camps, including Auschwitz, and both saw and experienced unspeakable atrocities, all of which he described in a tear-filled interview.

After liberation from Dachau in 1945, Ross went to a displaced persons camp and then to America with the aid of the U.S. Committee for Orphaned Children, which found safe places for the young survivors. He ended up at Boston's Jewish Family and Children's Service in 1948, which sent him to Windsor Mountain in 1949 because "the agency believed the school was a good place where children from Europe would get individual attention and a good education," said Ross. "Max and Gertrud…were angels—they saved me," he said.

Eventually earning three degrees, Ross spent forty years as a psychologist and social worker in Boston's inner-city public schools. Along with his son, Michael, a Boston city councilor, he is credited with establishing both the New England Holocaust Memorial and the Boston Holocaust Museum. In 2009, at his home in Newton, Massachusetts, Ross shared his story:

RC: Stephan, can you tell me a little about where you came from and your parents?

SR: I was born in Lodz, Poland. We were eight children…very poor, no toilets. My father was selling kosher meat; he was very religious. We had no education, but my mother would tell me, "Szmulek, you're going to be a great man." My parents gave me to a Christian family to be safe from the Nazis. The Germans came into the town, and they burned peoples' beards in the street with their cigarettes. Nothing should be forgotten, nothing…They should have dropped the atomic bomb on the Germans.

They took me to the woods to be safe. Some Polish people—you can count on your fingers—they helped. Then later, I pretended to be Polish. But the Germans didn't believe me, and they kicked me, beat me, pulled my pants down and brought me to a camp. In that camp, I found my brother. It was survival of the fittest; I survived by my instincts.

I was liberated from Dachau on April 29, 1945, with thirty-two thousand other inmates. What I want to tell you was that it was not a miracle; it was the might of the American armies. I was in the Valley of Death. It's not easy to tell how I got out from over there.

RC: What happened after you got to Windsor Mountain?

SR: I was mentally not together. I couldn't study or learn, and Gertrud picked me up. The agency didn't want me to stay there [Windsor Mountain]; *they said I wasn't high school material. So I went and spoke to Gertrud. She gave me, always, a session. She said, "You will do well, you will do well." She said, "You can stay with us here, and we will do what we can to get you to graduate." I wanted to be like her, the compassion, the sensitivity, the care. She said to me that I will do well, and she said, "Your mother knew what she was saying, that you will someday be a great man."*
RC: Were there other survivors there?

SR: Uh, Feiga, Heinz, Harry, me—maybe five, maybe eight. [Franny Hall recalled that there were seven children there who survived the Holocaust. She said, "There was little Harry, twelve years old, who wouldn't talk at first. Everyone cried at a faculty meeting one day because the art teacher came in and said, 'Harry drew a picture and spoke today.' They would hide buns in their pockets out of fear of hunger."]

RC: What else do you remember about Windsor?

SR: Heinz was intelligent, the brave warrior for the family. It is not possible to find a family like this, with such zest for healing and the environment that they set up to make a better world for people. Love. Affection. Gertrud was so pretty, wearing the high heels, and she still had a beautiful figure…when she was a lot older than she looked.

RC: Was there anything you were not happy about?

SR: There were some kids, decent kids, who got involved in sex and had children. Some of the kids should have been sent home to bring a message to others. Some did go home; some got married. They didn't always send them home because they [the kids] *would say, "We liked each other. I didn't do it violently, so we had a baby." This was not an easy task to overcome* [in a co-ed school] *with boys being attracted to girls, and girls being attracted to boys.* [One source noted that teachers were known to take girls to Albany, where Heinz would often pay for their abortions.]

WINDSOR MOUNTAIN SCHOOL OPENS ITS DOORS EVEN FURTHER

African Americans, like Maurice Eldridge and the Crockett children, and white activists, like the Wilkinsons and Durrs, along with survivors of the Nazi death camps, all found in Windsor Mountain School a safe and nurturing home. And in 1956, still others came.

Five Hungarian students who had fled from a short-lived revolt against the Soviet communist invasion of their country were introduced in a January

11, 1957 *Berkshire Eagle* article titled "Russian Language Is Shelved by Five Hungarian Students." All five were granted full scholarships at Windsor Mountain, and a sixth student transferred from Berkshire School because of Windsor's more concentrated English-teaching program and flexible schedule. It was also reported that on "Wednesday afternoon, the group, accompanied by the Rev. Robert S.S. Whitman, rector of Trinity Parish, went to Dee's Department Store to purchase clothing."

Eldridge said that there was a softening of the tensions that had existed between the school and the town as both worked together to help settle the refugees. This cooperation was mentioned in a May 21, 1957 *Eagle* article titled "Lenox Church Sponsors $5,000 County Drive to Help Pay for Schooling of Hungarians." Also noted was the school's enrollment that year: 137.

In the early to mid-'60s, diversity and the Windsor scholarship program expanded even further, according to a May 4, 1964 *Berkshire Eagle* article titled "7 Birmingham Negroes to Attend Windsor Mountain School in Lenox." The article stated, "Windsor Mountain School has accepted seven young Negroes from the Birmingham, Ala., area for entrance next fall, all of them A students...[They] were interviewed by a traveling talent scout working for the 30 schools affiliated with Project ABC [A Better Chance]."[95]

Windsor Mountain, under Heinz Bondy's leadership, was a founding member of the ABC Project, sponsored by the Office of Economic Opportunity. Initiated in 1963, the project enabled academically talented inner-city and southern youth to attend one of the independent schools that signed on to the program in response to John F. Kennedy's call for equal access for minority youth to the nation's top schools. Many of these students went on to distinguished careers, among them Massachusetts governor Deval Patrick, who attended Milton Academy in Milton, Massachusetts. Bill Dobbs recalled that Windsor's Eagle chapter of CORE (Congress on Racial Equality) and its faculty advisor, Wallace Roberts (1962–64), a volunteer during Freedom Summer 1964, raised money so the seven Birmingham students could attend the school.

The ABC program ran a second year at Windsor, according to the *Eagle* of March 5, 1966, which, in an article titled "A Better Chance in Berkshire," noted that twenty students would be attending one of four participating Berkshire boarding schools. The arrival of the ABCers, while welcomed by the Windsor community, resulted in the school's costs greatly increasing because, like the more prosperous African elites that Heinz had recruited in the early '60s, these students, too, would receive full scholarships in addition to clothing and spending money. This remarkable generosity on the part of the Bondys—generosity, it would turn out, they couldn't afford—would later figure into the school's serious financial problems. One alumnus questioned whether this was, in fact, generosity or just poor financial management in terms of spending more than the school could manage.

UTOPIAN POSSIBILITIES: ALUMNI IN THEIR OWN WORDS: RICHARD NEELY, '60

Richard Neely and Bob Neaman, '62, spoke in utopian terms about the faculty and staff at Windsor Mountain and the way it was in the late '50s and early '60s.

Neely, who still practices law and served as justice and chief justice of the West Virginia Court of Appeals, wrote on the Windsor discussion site on November 21, 2009, about coming to Windsor Mountain in 1956, when there were about seventy-four students:

> *I saw it* [Windsor] *in the post–World War II days, when Victorian morality and single-sex prep schools were the norm elsewhere, and then I saw it after the sexual revolution and the drug revolution and the co-ed revolution. I can tell you that in my day, Windsor was substantially more intellectually vibrant than Dartmouth College* [where Neely was an undergraduate]. *But that was because notwithstanding the "progressive" nature of the education, we had real order and structure as well as good faculty.*
>
> *In the years that I was a student, a very high percentage of our students came from families of European refugees, academics, genuine enthusiasts for progressive education and certified liberals. When Heinz interviewed me in 1954 at my house, my father asked Heinz what he thought of Senator Joe McCarthy. Heinz tried to say something tactful like, "Well, we let the students make up their own minds about subjects like that," at which point my father pressed him for his personal opinion. Heinz said he thought McCarthy was a disgrace to the United States Senate, at which point my father said, "Well, that's the school for Richard!" There was no force-feeding of classical music, classical literature or other high culture because a large portion of the students brought that culture with them. They also listened to Elvis Presley and danced in the rec room, but there*

was no resistance to high culture and doing plays like The Seagull [one of dozens of plays directed by Franny Hall].

My two sons went to the Buxton School in Williamstown, which in many ways is like the Windsor of yore. But I didn't think that their education came close to approaching in quality the education I got at Windsor in the 1950s. Part of that is that it is no longer possible to avoid television-like diversions (DVD's, etc.) and other intrusions of popular culture, but another part of it is that the teachers simply didn't have the same depth of background as our teachers like Jim, Franny, Label, Oldrick Prohaska [sic]. Once, long after I had graduated, Oldrick asked me if I had ever seen his correspondence with [noted economist] John Maynard Keynes during the 1930s and then promptly brought out a box of letters he and Keynes had exchanged!

ALUMNI IN THEIR OWN WORDS: BOB NEAMAN, '62

Robert Gordon Neaman (1943–2012) took pride in carrying on the Bondys' educational mission. "It was half social work, half teaching," he said of the alternative school in Westchester County where he guided young people. Later, he went to White Plains High School as a counselor, and when he died of lung cancer, a colleague there, Elaine Norelli, wrote of him: "You were a guiding force to both teachers and students. You touched more people than you will ever know." In 2011, Bob generously shared his memories of Windsor Mountain:

RC: How did you happen to go to Windsor Mountain?

RN: My parents [Bob's father went to Harvard Law School and was an attorney for CBS] *were looking around for a boarding school. I was kind of rebellious and was not doing well in school. When I got there* [Windsor] *the first day, I was nervous, but right away everybody was so friendly. I don't know; it's hard to describe.*

RC: What about the nature of the education?

RN: Small classes—Franny's English class may have been fifteen. [We] *called teachers by their first name; they taught all about trust. Gertrud would give these lectures, and there was Milan, head of maintenance. Every afternoon, I would find him and we'd build something or I'd be on the big tractor mowing the lawns. And I could drive his personal truck. That was a great privilege. He was like a second father. He could make anything: tables, bookcases, anything. I have some. He was really unbelievable.*

Mama Milan would come to your room and look, and if she didn't like what she saw, she would dump the wastebasket onto your bed. She would take the dresser and dump all the clothes on the floor. The mattresses would be on the floor, and you would have to start from scratch and re-do it. But everybody loved her. She'd hug every kid every day, you know. [Linda Fields described the same scene when referring to the day she learned that "there was no maid service at Windsor Mountain School!"]

RC: You said that when you were at Windsor ['59–62], *it was very different from the way it was in the '70s. How was it different?*

RN: The school got crazy in the '70s. Here's an example: I said to a guy who was there later, "Didn't you love the place?" He said, "I don't remember anything, we were so stoned." And the kids were sleeping with each other, and the teachers were sleeping with the kids—it was just…I think he [Heinz] *lowered the standards. I mean, he was just taking anybody to make money.*

We had diverse students—some on scholarship, one from the Deep South who went to Harvard and became an important journalist, wealthy kids, kids from Africa and Germany and Max Jacobson's daughter, Jill, who was in my class. Jacobson was Gertrud's doctor. He kept President Kennedy awake for days on end with his "magic elixir," mostly amphetamines, when Kennedy went to Moscow for Khrushchev. And he would bring up Eddie Fisher [the singer and one of Jacobson's patients] *in his private plane to Pittsfield when he came to visit. One time, Jacobson brought Johnny Mathis, who sang for us. Gertrud loved him; she used to call him Mr. Marcus. She never looked at a TV. She knew nothing about popular culture, just kids. So Gertrud said, "Oh, Mr. Fisher, are you married?" And it was that time of Eddie and his divorce from Elizabeth Taylor—everybody knew. He loved her because she didn't know who he was. She just accepted him for him.*

And Adrienne Belafonte was here. Heinz said to us before Harry [Belafonte] *came up for Parents' Weekend, "Please don't ask for autographs; leave him alone. Let him just be a father." He came up in this big Cadillac with a white chauffeur, I remember. And that silver suit with a beautiful white shirt that was open—he was the most beautiful man. And then later, Eleanor Bondy would visit him when she was in New York.*

RC: What was the relationship between the town and the school?

RN: Well, all we could do was go into Lenox in the afternoon to the Wendover for a hamburger or a soda, you know, where the Shear Design is now, across from the Village Inn. And on weekends, we could take the bus to Pittsfield to the movies and to the Chinese restaurant [the China Clipper], *and we went to Hagyard's, the drugstore across from the grocery store.*[96] *And when I was driving the truck around, Larry* [McCormick] *and I would go to Joe's Diner* [in Lee].

There's one store we couldn't go into because they had been not nice to some of the kids, about race or something. So Heinz said, "We will boycott; we won't ever go to that store." [In a speech he gave at Swarthmore College, Maurice Eldridge, who is African American, told of a boycott, which might be the one to which Neaman was referring. Eldridge told of experiencing his "first taste of activism" when a local barber told him that he didn't "cut my kind of hair." Eldridge reported the experience to Heinz Bondy, "[and] we boycotted the barber for the next three years." On the other hand, Haldor Reinholt, a math teacher at Windsor a few years later (and whose wife, Genia, was a Windsor housemother), told of a business that he admired for its tolerance. He said, "Lenox was then a conservative town with prejudices against anything that was different. Long hair was looked down on. But one person was friendly: Mr. Gregory of Gregory's Market, now O'Brien's Market next to the gas station, Hoff's. He was wonderful. When the kids would steal beer, he never reported it to the police. He always called Heinz to say, 'It happened again. Can you clamp down a little bit, you know?'"]

There was some resentment from the townies, but once, when there was almost a fight, we said to them, "No, we're not all rich kids; kids are here on scholarship. We don't want to wear this jacket and tie, but we have to—it's a rule." Anyway, we became kind of friends with them. [Rob

Putnam, who attended Windsor a few years after Neaman and who is now a school superintendent, recalled another scenario. He said there was once "a fight, where all the kids went racing out of Windsor Mountain to get into it."]

RC: So what was it about Windsor, Bob, that you would say had the greatest impact?

RN: I don't know—just to experience Gertrud and the teachers. It's hard to explain to people why this school meant so much to us. I mean, it's still the biggest thing in my life.

The year that Bob Neaman graduated, 1962, also marked a utopian milestone for Windsor's diverse soccer team. On November 26, 1962, the *Berkshire Eagle* published an article titled "Windsor Mt. Establishes Four Firsts":

The Windsor Mountain soccer team established four firsts in taking the Western New England Preparatory Soccer Association championship. Windsor Mountain was the first co-educational school, the first school in Berkshire County, the first unbeaten team and the first school with less than 200 boys to win the crown.

Besides American players, there were students from Mexico, Ghana, Kenya, Japan and India. John Mwangi, one of the Kenyans, "obviously had a past but kept it to himself," wrote Peter Roeper, a teammate. It was rumored that the big dent in his head had come from fighting in Mau Mau pro-independence wars in Kenya. When Stan Joseph, a retired psychologist, met Mwangi in 1964, he said Mwangi told him that he had been a student at Windsor Mountain, made possible by Kenyan official Tom Mboya, who sponsored the African Student Airlifts in the early '60s that gave hundreds of African students (including Barack Obama's father) a chance to study at schools in the United States.

Another Kind of Growth: New Buildings on Campus (and Two in Ashes)

With growth in numbers of students (by 1958, there were 145) came new construction. Included with an article in the January 18, 1958 *Berkshire Eagle* titled "Windsor Mt. School Opens New Gym" were pictures of the inside and outside of the new "modern-design wooden gymnasium." Before the gym's completion, Windsor Mountain had used the facilities of its neighbors, Lenox High School and the Lenox School for Boys.

Around the time that the new gym was completed, a building used by Windsor Mountain as a dormitory and art studio went up in flames. The fire was apparently caused by a student, according to Mike Cunningham, the current property manager. It had once been a garage and barn when part of

An impromptu jam session on the back porch of the dining hall at Windsor. *From 1969 Windsor yearbook.*

Major George E. Turnure's estate, Beaupre, which Windsor had purchased in 1956.[97] Another fire on March 3, 1961, destroyed the beautiful thirty-two-room mansion on the Beaupre property that Windsor had been using for a dormitory. Students had to be boarded out for the remainder of the school term until two buildings went up "in record time" before the opening of school in September 1961. The article "Dormitories Opening at Windsor Mountain," printed in the September 9, 1961 *Berkshire Eagle*, carried this brief description: "[A] feature of the opening of Windsor Mountain School next Sunday will be two new cement-block dormitories [one for boys, one for girls], situated in pine groves and with designs that are hallmarked with simplicity," a euphemism, some alumni said, referring to the barracks-like design of the buildings.

In June 1960, between the time the new gym and dormitories were built, the Bondys celebrated a new dining hall, "a pre-fab job," added onto the south side of the administration building, the main manse, and extending from the lobby. It had a twenty-five- by six-foot patio and a stairway on each side at the southern end of the building. The grounds around the building were landscaped with evergreens, mock orange plants and crabapple trees, all donated by the 1960 graduating senior class.[98]

Added to this mix of two new dorms, a new dining hall and a gymnasium was still another new building, a combination auditorium and theater with a hall for exhibiting art. The *Berkshire Eagle*'s June 6, 1964 article "Friendship Started in Concentration Camp to Lead to New Building at Windsor Mtn." reported that Dr. Max Jacobson had allegedly made a promise to a concentration camp inmate, whose wife was about to have a baby, that he would take care of their child, which he did, including eventually sending him to Windsor Mountain School. Because Jacobson believed the school had helped the troubled boy, the doctor and his wife, Nina, sought a way to help Windsor Mountain. Thus, in a brief ceremony on June 5, 1964, the auditorium—a gift from Jacobson—was formally dedicated to Nina, with Broadway actor Roscoe Brown performing a dramatic reading of poetry. The expected completion date was late September or early October at an estimated cost of $100,000. Lesley Larsen Albert said that Jacobson had intended to pay for the theater with proceeds from his investment in the play *On a Clear Day You Can See Forever*, but "it flopped, and Heinz and the school ended up having to pay for the building," which was "another nail in the financial coffin of the school."

Windsor's graduation speaker that spring, according to a June 8, 1964 *Berkshire Eagle* article titled "Windsor Mtn. Graduates 66," was civil

Modern theater building at Windsor Mountain. *Author's collection.*

The Bondy/Roeper/Wiener family's annual Christmas gathering. *Courtesy of the Roeper family.*

rights proponent, former U.S. senator and Democratic congressman Claude Pepper of Florida. In his speech, he "stressed the importance of having social progress equal technological progress." He also told the students, "The aim of world peace should be carried out by every human being."

CHRISTMAS AT WINDSOR MOUNTAIN SCHOOL

While Windsor Mountain School changed from decade to decade, affected by the social, economic and political changes taking place in the world around it, certain things stayed exactly the same, the case in point being the family's tradition of gathering at Windsor Mountain for the Christmas holiday. Jenny Roper, who, like other family members, came every year to the Berkshires, described one of the traditions they shared on the eve before the holiday:

> *Gertrud took utmost care with Christmas formalities. In the wood-paneled library with floor-to-ceiling windows stood a huge Christmas tree. All around the room were presents piled high on tables. Before anyone was allowed to see the huge, decorated, brightly lit tree, everyone first had to stand outside the closed library doors. A piano stood at the entrance, and Gertrud would begin playing carols. Then, with much pomp and circumstance, and at the precise moment that Gertrud decided, the doors would open. Then all were allowed to enter and view the gorgeous setting.*

"Awful Awful" milkshake glass from Friendly's Restaurant, a favorite eatery of Windsor students. *Author's collection.*

122

A huge dinner would follow. Gertrud's grandniece Ellen Winner (now a psychology professor in the same field, gifted education, as Gertrud's daughter, Annemarie) came to those dinners with her family every year as a child and remembered something her great-aunt said, which she thought was quite funny then: "Scratch your plates, children." (She really meant for them to *scrape* their plates clean.) "My cousins [the Roepers and the Gerards] and I had a grand time living in the students' dorm rooms, roaming the kitchen at night and raiding the industrial-size fridge, ice-skating on the pond and going to Friendly's to get an Awful, Awful."

So it seems that during the '50s and early '60s, Windsor Mountain was, in many ways, a kind of utopian Oz—not just for students but also for young family members, who to this day carry vivid memories of the huge gray stone manse where they'd climb the beautiful mahogany stairway to their bedrooms, replete with marble fireplaces and the loveliest views of the Berkshire Hills in winter.

Chapter 6

Windsor Attracts Prominent Families, from Monk and Belafonte to Shultz

I loved the politics, the teachers, the independence. I feel WMS had a powerful effect on who I am today, what I believe, how I teach and how I run my foundation.
—*Adrienne Belafonte Biesemeyer, e-mail, January 18, 2013*

Why did so many African American jazz greats, performers and athletes, as well as other prominent families, send their children to Windsor Mountain School? In some cases, the answer has to do with its location in the Berkshires, a mecca for the arts and a place of natural beauty all year round. "Like a dream in the night/as the snow settles white/there's a fire burning bright/in Massachusetts," wrote folksinger Arlo Guthrie, capturing the essence of the area where he went to school and now lives.

Renowned jazz pianist and composer Thelonius Monk (1917–1982), father of bebop, and Randy Weston (1926–), who studied with Monk and went on to international fame, might have first learned about Windsor Mountain when they performed at the Music Inn (1950–79) in Lenox and taught at the Lenox School of Jazz (1957–60). Both the inn and the school were the creations of Stephanie and Philip Barber, who, along with subsequent owners of the inn, brought dozens of the most famous folk, blues and jazz performers in the country to Lenox.[99]

The Music Inn and Windsor Mountain School—both located not far from the Boston Symphony Orchestra's summer home, Tanglewood— shared a similar life span, and both brought to Lenox the kind of diversity unusual for that time and place. And Windsor students, like Jean (Mercier) Whitehead and Gigi Buffington, would return in the summer to work at the inn or Windsor Mountain, where many of the Tanglewood music students were housed.

While performing in the Berkshires, Monk and Weston might have heard that Windsor Mountain welcomed African American students when most other private boarding schools were still single-sex and not as integrated or as progressive as Windsor. And they might have been attracted by the school's fine arts curriculum. However it happened, both Monk's son, Thelonius Jr. (aka TM or "Toot"), '69, now a jazz drummer, and his younger sister, Barbara ("Boo Boo"), who sang on albums with her brother (and who died of breast cancer in 1984), went to Windsor Mountain along with Niles "Azzedine" Weston, a jazz percussionist who at one time traveled with his father as a cultural ambassador under the U.S. State Department. (Christopher Smith, '70, said that for a brief time, he and Azzedine were roommates when they first arrived at Windsor in 1967, and he remembered Monk putting on concerts in the dining hall for Windsor students.)

Robin Kelley, Thelonius Monk's biographer, interestingly reveals a completely different explanation about how TM Jr. got to Windsor Mountain:

> Toot...transferred to Kingsley Hall [1957–67], a boarding school in Great Barrington, MA...During his year at Kingsley Hall, he joined the basketball team and learned about some of the other neighboring prep schools...One school, in particular, Windsor Mountain, in nearby Lenox, MA, caught his attention. Or more accurately, one girl caught his attention. Her name was Adrienne Belafonte...Toot promptly applied to Windsor Mountain. "Of course, I did not know that Adrienne was a senior. So when I got there the next year, she's gone. Her little sister, Shari, was there, but she's twelve years old." But Randy Weston's son, Azzedine, was also there, and Boo joined him the same year.[100]

Adrienne Belafonte, the eldest daughter of actor, singer and humanitarian Harry Belafonte and his first wife, Marguerite Byrd, a psychologist, learned about Windsor Mountain School when she was a camper in the summer of 1962 at Franny and Jim Hall's Windsor Camp, located on the Windsor campus for six summers (1957–63). "I chose to attend the school, and my folks let me," wrote Adrienne.

In his autobiography, Harry Belafonte wrote:

I exercised the right I'd retained in our divorce to say where the girls would go to school, and sent both Shari [born 1954] and Adrienne [born 1949] to a boarding school in Lenox, Massachusetts, called Windsor Mountain. It got them away from their meddlesome grandmother [Marguerite's mother, whom, he said, was trying to turn his daughters against him], *yet was close enough that I could drive up to see them on weekends. As I did, I fell in love with the region and bought a 180-acre hilltop farm in Chatham, New York, in between Manhattan and the school, so we could spend cozy country weekends as a family.*[101]

Heinz recalled that when Harry visited Adrienne at Windsor Mountain, he would sometimes play touch football on the lawn and sign autographs and take her out with a group of her friends for something to eat. And he'd often go into the kitchen at Windsor to chat and laugh with the mostly African American cooks and compliment their work.

Adrienne noted that when she started at Windsor in 1962, she was one of 6 students in the school's eighth grade. There were 75 in the school then, but by the time she left in 1967, there were more than 150. "My one true sadness," she wrote, "is that the school enlarged enrollment and took in way too many students. [That] took away some of the intimacy of the education. And I feel that that and funding was the reason for its demise—a real catch-22." She said she loved the school, the faculty and the "exuberant students who deeply cared about a world they knew little about. My first year, the senior class rode freedom buses to the South to help rebuild a burned church, I think, or a home."

Adrienne settled in West Virginia, where, Harry said, her "mixed marriage [to David Biesemeyer] didn't raise an eyebrow."[102] She had two children, Rachel Blue and Brian; started a private family counseling practice; and, later, with her daughter, founded the Anir Foundation (1997), which focuses on assisting South Africans with housing, education, HIV/AIDS education and prevention and other health issues related to women and their families.[103]

Shari Belafonte, five years younger than Adrienne, came to Windsor Mountain when she was twelve but was allowed to skip grades, entering as a ninth grader in 1967, the year Adrienne was finishing. However, Shari stayed for only one year. She wrote, "[I loved] Lenox and a horse farm up the road, where I would walk to and then ride a half-blind little mare almost every day." But in the year she was there, "the kids set the lab on fire, and one died...[and] I had a nasty fracture from skiing at night

Adrienne Belafonte dancing around the Maypole at the annual May Fair celebration at Windsor Mountain. *From 1967 Windsor yearbook.*

with Haldor [the skiing and math teacher] at Brodie. My parents dragged me out of there…They freaked over my smoking pot, breaking my leg and having schoolmates doing drugs." (The Belafontes were not alone in deciding to withdraw their child from Windsor for similar reasons.)

Shari finished up at Buxton, a progressive school in Williamstown, Massachusetts, and then went to college, modeled and acted. She would go on to grace the covers of some three hundred fashion and beauty magazines, including *Playboy*.[104] She said that she is now "acting when I can and shooting photography and video on different projects in California." "Til this day," she wrote, "I still dream about being [at Windsor] in the snow, on the front lawn at night. It was so dreamlike. There's a quick scene in a Nick Cage/Tea Leoni movie where the snow is falling from the heavens. It looked like that."

Harry Belafonte's longtime friendship with Sidney Poitier (they met as nineteen-year-olds in 1945) might be how Beverly Poitier, the eldest daughter of Sidney and his first wife, came to attend Windsor Mountain. (According to Congressman Chris Gibson, from Kinderhook, New York, Poitier, like Belafonte, also had a home in the Hudson Valley of upstate New York.) There, from 1966 to 1970, Beverly wrote about Windsor in a brief online bio: "I attended a very liberal boarding school, Windsor Mountain, in Lenox, Massachusetts…We learned early on that the world was, indeed, small and that we were in effect a global village."[105]

The day Martin Luther King Jr. was killed, "Beverly was rehearsing a play," remembered Franny Hall, "and someone came into the theater and announced, 'Someone shot MLK.' Beverly became hysterical and could not be consoled."

Jean Whitehead said she and Beverly were both in a play during the Parents' Weekend/May Fair celebration, when Sidney was in the audience. "And, you know," said Jean, "[we just thought] that was normal. The poor guy was probably bored out of his mind." Cameron Melville, '70–71, was "heart-struck" when he heard that Poitier, the first black actor to win an Academy Award (*Lilies of the Field*) was about to arrive. "I loved him; I was wild about him…I think he had done *To Sir with Love*, which was a big deal at the time."

Beverly, now a writer, jewelry designer and screenwriter, lives in Atlanta, Georgia.

Karen Pamela Smythe attended Windsor Mountain from 1960 to 1964. She was the daughter of an African American couple, Drs. Hugh H. and Mabel M. Smythe (Haith), both of whom were teachers, writers and diplomats.[106] Hugh Smythe (1913–1977), ambassador to Syria (1965–67)

John Campanella on the lawn at Windsor Mountain with Eric Waggoner in Shakespeare's *A Midsummer Night's Dream. Courtesy of Franny Hall.*

and Malta (1967–69), had worked with **W.E.B. Du Bois** at the NAACP and as a secretary to Langston Hughes, while Mabel Smythe (1918–2006) had assisted Thurgood Marshall in preparing the *Brown v. Board of Education* case and eventually served as ambassador to Cameroon and Equatorial Guinea.

It's unclear how Dinah "Queen" Washington (1924–1963), pop, gospel and jazz singer, learned of Windsor, but two of her sons (from different marriages), George Kenneth Jenkins (born 1946) and Robert Grayson (born 1949), attended Windsor Mountain for a year. (Her seventh and last husband was Dick "Night Train" Lane, the well-known football player.) In her biography of Washington, Nadine Cohodas wrote:

> *Dinah enrolled George* [seventeen] *and Bobby* [fourteen] *in the pricey Windsor Mountain School in Lenox, MA* [September 1963]. *Tuition, including fees for each was $2600, which Dinah was paying on the installment plan. They were not the only black students at the school, but*

they were in a distinct minority. The boys were among the best athletes, though, and Bobby loved being something of a star on the sports teams.[107]

When Dinah died in Detroit on December 14, 1963, at the age of thirty-nine, the boys returned to Windsor in January 1964, a month after their mother's death, to finish the school year. But they would not go back to the school the following year, "given the high tuition and their unsettled financial situation."[108]

Joni Campanella Roan graduated from Windsor Mountain in 1964 and her brother, John, in 1971. Both were the children of Dodger Hall of Famer and civil rights pioneer Roy Campanella (1921–1993), who became a quadriplegic as the result of an automobile accident and eventually a champion for people with disabilities. In 1964, by then in a wheelchair and divorced, Roy married Roxie Doles, a widow, and adopted her two children, Joni and John.[109]

Joni now helps to run the foundation founded by her late mother, the Roy and Roxie Campanella Physical Therapy Scholarship Endowment, Northridge Foundation. And John, whom Franny Hall remembers acting in her plays, works with a North Hollywood security firm and is a coach for youth baseball.

OTHER PROMINENT FAMILIES ATTRACTED TO WINDSOR MOUNTAIN

Children from prominent families came to Windsor Mountain School for many of the same reasons as other students: because of their family circumstances, because their needs weren't being met within more traditional schools or because they had heard of Windsor's nurturing environment and beautiful setting. Included among them was Alma Tuchman, '66, daughter of historian Barbara Tuchman (*The Guns of August*); Tom Gibson, son of playwright William Gibson (*The Miracle Worker* and *Two for the Seesaw*) and his wife, Margaret Brenman-Gibson (biographer of Clifford Odets), who lived in nearby Stockbridge; and David Agronsky, '65, son of journalist Martin Agronsky.

Anne Hemenway, '71, daughter of Russell D. Hemenway (1926–2014), director of the liberal National Committee for an Effective Congress (funded in 1948 by Eleanor Roosevelt), is carrying on the work of her father, who was described as "a true warrior spirit in American politics."[110]

Barbara Lennox Shultz (White), who became a teacher, graduated from Windsor in '74 and is a daughter of George Shultz (born 1920), former U.S. secretary of state, secretary of labor and secretary of the treasury, who summers with his family in Cummington, Massachusetts, in Hampshire County, in the foothills of the Berkshires.[111]

Brother and sister Mike and Holly Stern, from a family with historic connections to the area, both attended Windsor Mountain. After their parents, Helen Burroughs Sedgwick and Henry Dwight Sedgwick, divorced, their mother married Philip M. Stern, author and political aide and grandson of the founder of Sears, Roebuck and Co., who then adopted them. The family of their father, Henry Dwight Sedgwick, whom they share with half-sibling actress Kyra Sedgwick, goes back to eighteenth-century Stockbridge, Massachusetts, and lawyer Theodore Sedgwick, known for winning the 1781 case that freed Elizabeth Freeman, known as "Mum Bett." This was a landmark case that led to the outlawing of slavery in the state of Massachusetts, the first state to do so. Another ancestor, William Ellery Sedgwick, actually once owned the property that became Windsor Mountain School. He called his estate the Elms and lived there from 1856 to 1869.

Philip Stern was the speaker at his son Mike's 1971 graduation from Windsor Mountain, according to the June 7, 1971 *Berkshire Eagle* article titled "Push Reform, Author Tells Graduates of Windsor Mountain." Mike, who, said classmate Terry Hall, kicked "a pretty bad heroin habit," is now one of the best jazz guitarists in the country, whose career included being part of the band Blood, Sweat and Tears (1976) and playing and recording with Miles Davis (1981). Holly Stern, '72, is the mother of seven children that include five Nozuka brothers, all musicians, and their two sisters.

Bob Blafield, Windsor music teacher from 1969 to 1975, called Judy Collins's son, Clark Taylor, "a sad boy" but noted that he was bright and musical. Because of Clark's addiction to drugs and alcohol, Collins's attempt to find a boarding school that could address his problems was difficult. While he was attending a non-structured school in Vermont, she got a call to come there and bail him out of jail. The headmaster there told her about Windsor Mountain, which "worked well for young people who might have issues with substance abuse."[112] After meeting with Heinz Bondy, wrote Collins, "[we] were both encouraged by his openness about the problem of drugs. We felt the school, a stone structure with substance and history, would be good for Clark...But he was into drugs there as quickly as he unpacked his bags, and the experience resulted, a few months later, in Clark's first overdose. I drove to Lenox and found [him] waiting for me at the Pittsfield General Hospital."[113] This was in 1975, when Clark was sixteen. Windsor closed soon after that.

Clark eventually married and had a child but, after seven years of sobriety, relapsed into alcohol and committed suicide in 1992 at the age of thirty-three. Several alumni, among them Christopher Smith and Jean Whitehead, as well as faculty, including Haldor Reinholt, noted that there were several suicides by former students, who, after leaving Windsor, were able to sustain a good life for a while but in the end were conquered by their addictions. Certainly not every student flourished at Windsor Mountain, and Mac Benford said that he and other teachers suffered from feelings of failure as much as those students they could not help.

But for the most part, for children of prominent families, Windsor Mountain School was a place where they could be themselves without being singled out because of their names. Perhaps for these children, too, Windsor Mountain became a place of refuge, although the outside world was never far away.

Chapter 7

1965–74: Drugs, Sex and Rock-and-Roll: Windsor as a Reflection of the Times

The first half of [my novel] Riverfinger Women *takes place at Windsor Mountain, an adventuresome and exciting place to be, not just because of drugs, sex and rock 'n' roll—which were all there—but because of the kinds of relationships between students and between students and teachers, transformative relationships…I found a place full of people like me who had come there because they couldn't quite fit into other places.*
—*Elana Nachman Dykewomon, '67, in* Across Time and Space
(DVD, 2002)

Elana Dykewomon, a novelist and activist, portrays Windsor Mountain School and its leading figures in her "lesbian coming-of-age story." Anyone who knew the school and Gertrud and Heinz will immediately recognize them. In her book, Elana uses the name Inez Riverfinger. Gertrud is Theodora, Heinz is Harold, Max is Karl and Highland Hills, Windsor Mountain School, "no average New England boarding school," she writes as she [Inez] is ushered into "the solemn chambers of the eighty-year-old foundress, Theodora Koenig":

> *"Yah, now Karl he is dead these twenty years now. Yah, Karl is dead, but the meaning of his work, it is still living. Here at Highland Hills we vill not havf the free love, we vill not havf the marijuana…Sex, the sex, can be a good thing, but ve must understand it…Yah. So." Then Theodora would turn up her hearing aid and let you ask questions.*[114]

Nachman portrays Gertrud—whose daughter, Annemarie, described as liberal about sex—preaching caution, maybe because, at that time, many more students at Windsor were paying less attention to rules and giving in to the temptations of the sexual revolution, the proliferation of drugs and student rebellion across the country.

By the time Nachman graduated in '67, two major transitions were occurring: Gertrud, by then seventy-eight years old and afflicted with several medical problems, was withdrawing from the running of the school. Said Pamela Esler, "By 1972, Gertrud was literally cloistered in her apartment with a private nurse," though she continued to offer students advice and comfort whenever they came to see her. And second, the outside world had started to come in with a vengeance, and the "free love, the marijuana, the sex," all a part of the times, began to wreak havoc, causing a "breach in the trust between faculty and students," according to Bill Dobbs. And trust had been the mainstay of the Bondy philosophy. "Windsor had always wanted students to self-discipline, and now that approach didn't seem to be working anymore," echoed Christopher Smith. The Windsor of the late '60s and early '70s was not the Windsor of the '40s, '50s and early '60s.

ALUMNI IN THEIR OWN WORDS: JEANNIE (MERCIER) WHITEHEAD, '71

Jeannie Whitehead, who now lives in Great Barrington, Massachusetts, graduated from Windsor Mountain School in 1971 and met her husband, Peter, there:

> *I think everything that was going on at Windsor Mountain was going on everywhere else. In spite of the times and the drugs and the drinking and the promiscuity and all the rest that, again, was going on everywhere...there were people who were showing up every day with their hearts in the right place, wanting kids to succeed. So yes, we were sort of operating in this atmosphere where, on the one hand, the world was nuts but on the other hand, you still had to write your papers...And we had this physically beautiful campus. We'd have classes outdoors a lot, and we'd do these things called breakfast rides and go galloping through what's now Canyon Ranch and then come*

Anne Hemenway (left) and Jeannie (Mercier) Whitehead, roommates at Windsor Mountain, 1969. *Courtesy of Anne Hemenway.*

back to Kimball's Stables [now Kimball Farms, an assisted living residence], *and the family who owned the stables would have huge platters of scrambled eggs and bacon waiting for us. It was a lot of fun.*

People went skiing and hiking up Greylock, to New Hampshire and October Mountain and in Lenox up to Aspinwall Park, where there were trails. And there were a lot of plays and field trips. [We went] *to the Museum of Fine Arts in Boston for our art history class. And there were a lot of musicians at Windsor…Terry Hall would be playing drums, and a*

Student Jane Janson thanking Gertrud Bondy at graduation ceremonies. *From 1969 Windsor yearbook.*

guy named Dave Carter would be singing. And there were dance teachers, an arts studio and a major drama department. There were ski trips and, thanks to Haldor [Reinholt], an ice hockey team, co-ed. So I guess there was a certain real innocence at the same time as there were really sinister things going on; people were overdosing on heroin at the same time they were doing Chekhov plays with Franny.

You know, there were not a lot of rules and it could have been maybe stricter, and I don't think there was a lot of help in terms of applying to college. I mean, I can't say the school was responsible for that, but it didn't seem to be as structured as it might have been that way. But it gave me the more valuable thing, becoming curious about the world so you keep on learning on your own.

I was sort of caught off guard [at graduation]. First you go to Gertrud and shake her hand. And then you go around—there's like a little half-circle of the faculty, sitting in chairs—and you shake everyone's hand. And something about that exchange with her…it just sort of brought up all these feelings, and I was just crying the whole time.

DRUGS: KEEPING THE LID ON AT WINDSOR

Before "all hell broke loose" with drugs at Windsor Mountain—as Peter Whitehead described the late '60s—there was Max Jacobson (1900–1979). Prior to her taking methadone (which "for patients like Gertrud was legal but not always easy to secure," said Pamela Esler), Gertrud had sought relief for her angina pain with medication prescribed by Dr. Max Jacobson, who had fled Germany in 1936, the same year as Gertrud. Known as "Miracle Max" and dubbed "Dr. Feelgood" by the Secret Service because of the unorthodox medical treatments he administered to President John F. Kennedy, Jacobson—whose daughter, Jill, '66, attended Windsor Mountain—counted among his celebrity clients Elvis Presley, Anthony Quinn, Marilyn Monroe, Elizabeth Taylor, Tennessee Williams and Nelson Rockefeller. And he brought several with him to the school, including Eddie Fisher and Leontyne Price, who put on a benefit concert for Windsor Mountain.

President Kennedy, whose charisma and charm masked severe and lifelong back pain, found temporary relief with Jacobson's injections, and Jacobson traveled with the president to major summits, including a meeting with

Nikita Khrushchev in 1961, which science reporter Boyce Rensberger called "disastrous," noting that at the time, Kennedy might have been "high" on Max's remedy, which can cause "not only feelings of euphoria but also an exaggerated sense of power and superiority."[115] Jacobson, who also injected himself with his potpourri mixture, said his shots consisted of vitamins and hormones but were, in reality, mostly composed of addictive methamphetamines, or speed, along with vitamins, painkillers and human placenta, the negative effects of which included crashing and becoming disoriented.[116]

Jon Shapiro said, "Both teachers and parents were on Max's 'magic elixir,'" which Lesley Larsen Albert, owner of Loeb's Foodtown in Lenox, said was also referred to as "kickaboo bat juice, a baseball thing." Franny Hall said, "Almost everyone at Windsor Mountain in the '60s started taking his shots," including Eleanor (Heinz's first wife) and Heinz, who crashed his plane off Route 7 near the Pittsfield Airport "because," said Franny, "he was on speed," apparently taking it for back pain. One student noted that a syringe was found on the seat next to Heinz after the crash. According to an August 7, 1965 article in the *Berkshire Eagle* titled "Bondy Slightly Hurt in Light Plane Crash," Heinz was "reported to have asked, 'What did I do, black out?'" He was treated for a head cut at St. Luke's Hospital in Pittsfield and released.

Bob Neaman recalled, "Heinz got very sick once because he kept taking amphetamines when he was trying to stay up days on end to try to do college applications. He'd write all the letters to colleges. And he ended up in the hospital."

In 1969, when one of his patients died of "acute chronic intravenous amphetamine poisoning," Jacobson's practices were exposed, leading the New York Board of Regents to revoke his license in 1975 for prescribing amphetamines.[117]

Another incident related to drugs occurred three years later in 1968, but this one ended in a fatality, the worst tragedy ever to occur at Windsor Mountain. Doane Hulick's *Berkshire Eagle* article of April 22, 1968, "Night Fire in Unlocked Laboratory Kills Windsor Student," revealed how Richard Kauffmann, thirteen, and Derek DeVries entered Windsor's science building at 2:00 a.m. on April 20 to obtain the chemical toluol, a component of airplane glue, "to get high on." They lit a match, and the container exploded in Kauffmann's face. He died "at 9:15 AM in the Pittsfield General unit, BMC [Berkshire Medical Center]" of third-degree burns. DeVries survived. In another article about Windsor Mountain, appearing two years later in the same paper on December 5, 1970, Richard K. Weil wrote, "It would have been enough to drive other boarding schools out of business," but instead, the school's enrollments were way up, and "there was a waiting list of 150 for the 1970–71 year."[118]

Not long after that deadly accident, an article titled "Windsor Mt. School Sued by Dissatisfied Parent" appeared in the June 3, 1969 *Eagle*. The parent charged that "his minor son was 'exposed' to an 'unwholesome atmosphere' that included illegal use of drugs at the school." He sued for $3,000, the amount he had paid for tuition, room and board for a full year, though he took his son out of the school after two months, in November 1968.

Heinz tried to stem the tide of drug abuse, which ranged from pervasive use of marijuana to heroin and LSD, by issuing all kinds of warnings. In a letter included in the packet of information sent out to students before the opening of school in September 1969, he wrote, "The only way the school can be hurt from the outside is through use of drugs on the inside... It is, therefore, impossible for anyone in the school to use drugs without endangering its very existence." Christopher Smith said that at every evening assembly, Heinz would announce that police might be coming to raid the place. "He warned us so as to prevent the school from being closed down." (No one could recall there ever being a police raid.) Heinz's letter ended with: "It is essential...that you realize that you cannot remain at Windsor Mountain School if you use drugs."

The problem, according to several alumni, was that while there were, indeed, some students expelled for drug use, alcohol abuse and other offenses (and at least one faculty member was fired for alcohol, drugs and sex), the policy was not consistently or strictly enforced.[119] In fact, "not too many rules were enforced at Windsor," said Anne Hemenway. Mac Benford, who taught history at Windsor from 1964 to 1967 and who was elected by the students to be the faculty representative to the student court, said that he and Heinz were there to advise, although the court was endowed with the power to expel. "We cautioned them [the students on the court] that expulsion should be seen as the punishment of last resort," executed only after several warnings had been issued. Fred Burstein, '68, who went from being "a kid who quit school" to becoming the president of Windsor's student court, took seriously the power the court had to decide whether someone smoking pot should be given another chance. And Jeannie Whitehead, referring to the heroin problem, said that a few years later, "four kids did get kicked out, which was unusual. It got everyone's attention."

Heinz had difficulty giving up the school's philosophy, which held that the exercise of freedom would help students to become self-directing

Heinz Bondy in the library with members of the student court. *From 1968 Windsor yearbook.*

people. Was he unable to—or did he not believe he should—set more stringent limits when students broke the trust he offered them? The answer will differ depending on the person who is asked, but when Peter Whitehead was there, he observed, "Whenever a student was thrown out, Heinz would try to get them back in." Nate Steele quoted Heinz at the height of the drug problem as saying, "This [drug use] is illegal, but we're not policemen." He added, "They didn't turn over students' rooms. They wanted us to take responsibility for our own actions." As a result, however, Anne Hemenway thought some students got lost. "Perhaps there weren't enough ways for them to get help," she said. "Some people need more oversight at that age."

Besides the warnings Heinz issued about drug use and drug raids, there was another issue, as indicated in this letter to students in August 1970: "I am sorry to tell you that we must be very strict about pets in the dorm next school year. Last year the overflow of pets, dogs and cats especially (along with at least five other species), came to the attention of the Lenox Health Department...[The school could be] closed if we break their rules."

Cameron Melville said he remembered one dog, in particular, Farfel, who belonged to no one and to everyone: "He was sort of the school's mascot.

He'd wander the campus, and students would feed him LSD and everything else." And Pamela Esler described the time when Gerdi was making announcements in the theater at evening assembly and Farfel, unbeknownst to Gerdi, peed on the curtain.

Bob Blafield recalled the faculty meeting at which Heinz raised the pet issue, and during which "Heinz's dogs were under the table fighting." "The faculty," he said, "ignored Heinz's warning because they knew nothing would be done."

In addition to the tension between Windsor Mountain and the town's police and health departments, there were, according to Peter Whitehead and Terry Hall, "town/school tensions" in general. There were differences in class and race, and then there were the drugs. They noted that several of the Lenox locals saw longhaired students as hippies, and Terry Hall said Windsor kids were called "kooks." "We looked different," said Peter Whitehead. "We stood out. You couldn't go into town without getting into verbal confrontations. Heinz would tell us to be careful. 'Don't be stupid.' We didn't feel free to go anywhere."

Sex

Besides expelling some students for drug use, the student court was known to kick out a few of their peers "for sneaking into the girls' dorms," according to teacher Mac Benford. Bob Blafield said that there was also "a lot of sexual license, even between students and teachers." "Though Gertrud was liberal about sex," said Blafield, "it's not clear whether she approved of such couplings." Lesley Albert said, "Student-teacher sexual relationships were frowned upon." But Pamela Esler said they existed, noting one faculty member who would "make students his platonic or love slave—and did bed a few."

"Sex was no big deal at Windsor. Some said it was disgusting that teachers slept with students, but I just felt jealous. I didn't see it as a bad thing," said Roselle Van Nostrand. (While attending Windsor, Roselle fell in love with the Berkshires and returns with her son, Remy, every summer to do landscaping work.)

At the 2006 reunion, Esler said she heard one woman say, "There was a lot of sexual stuff that went on that shouldn't have." And regarding whether male faculty took advantage of female students, Esler said, "I know that they did, but [in some cases] it was an enriching experience."

"Such couplings," as Blafield called them, and the mixed reactions of alumni to these faculty-student relationships, were not uncommon at private schools in the '60s, as exemplified in an article in the *New York Times* in the spring of 2012 that exposed "sex abuse" at the prestigious (and, at the time, all-male) Horace Mann School in the Bronx.[120] Tek Young Lin, a former English teacher at Horace Mann, was quoted as saying, "In those days, it was very spontaneous and casual, and it did not seem really wrong," though the reporter concludes the article with Lin's acknowledgement that he might have crossed a line. And said Gary Alan Fine, a 1968 graduate of Horace Mann, "I can't imagine that in the late nineteen sixties anyone would have been terribly surprised had they learned that some faculty were having sexual relations with students…[It] was the way of the world."[121]

"Sex was always an issue," said Jonathan Shapiro. "There were two pump houses on the property—one to keep the property going and the other, where we went to smoke pot and have sex. People would go off and have sex all over the extensive grounds. It was said that if you walked around the grounds on a warm evening, you would trip over someone." A few alumni mentioned one student who was "infamous for impregnating two girls." "Yeah, there were abortions," said Lesley Larsen, who followed her mother as nurse at Windsor (and whose father drove Windsor's school bus and coached.) "I didn't give out any contraception, nor did my mother. But I'm not convinced that Gertrud didn't 'cause I remember she used to say, 'Don't forget to wear your rubbers.'"

ROCK-AND-ROLL

Terry Hall, now a full-time musician, went to Windsor Mountain, as did his brother, Parnee, '62, a prolific author of mysteries, because both of their parents, Franny and Jim Hall, taught there. Said Terry:

> *I was there at a time that was a turning point, 1969. Kids coming up from inner-city metropolitan areas brought "good things" like music, blues, Jimi Hendrix. They were ahead culture-wise, which led to exciting times* [and many helped raise Windsor's basketball scores], *but they also brought "bad things" like drugs, and some were heroin addicts.*

> *You'd walk around campus, and every room was blasting something different. Bands formed on campus, and I played the drums in some of them. My first band, Goody Twoshoes and the Filthy Beast, was ahead of its time. We played for dances at schools like Lenox High School, and at the Boys Club in Pittsfield, where we competed in the Battle of the Bands and won that competition.*

Terry mentioned Mike Stern's trio and Don Plange, '66, one of the Ghanaian soccer players who sang with Terry's band. A.B. Taylor, '71, an African American student from Pittsfield whose father, John Amos, was a chef at Windsor Mountain, also played guitar and is still a musician today. For many years part of the band Shenandoah, Terry toured with Arlo Guthrie and is still riding the big bus with him. They first met when Terry's brother, Parnee, was working with movie director and Stockbridge resident Arthur Penn on the film *Alice's Restaurant* and got Terry in the film as an extra. (Fred Burstein remembered Guthrie coming to Windsor to get extras for the film.) Besides touring with Guthrie, Terry, aka Terry a la Berry, continues writing songs and performing for and with children.

ACTIVISM AND APATHY

Students responded differently to the protest movements of the late '60s and early '70s. Some became activists, deciding they wanted to be part of changing the world; others dropped out. Anne Hemenway spoke of the dilemma facing students then: "We were trying to transcend the terrible tragedies we'd all lived through as a country (two Kennedy assassinations, MLK's, plus Vietnam). You know, there was just this sense of not really knowing as a teenager how really to take that on, and feeling somewhat overwhelmed by it all."

Christopher Smith, now owner of a printing business, said, "The air got let out of the balloon. It was the hopelessness because of the war and the times—not just the drugs. There wasn't the same seriousness and community. Heinz talked about the apathy. My class was pure apathy. But then again, we went to Pittsfield to protest and to D.C., where I got tear-gassed."

Despite the social upheaval, noted Hemenway, "there was a desire for civic action and responsibility. The teachers had it; we had it." And Zuzana Wiener, teacher and house parent, said, "Those times weren't as terrible as you might think. There was a special energy, an anti-Vietnam spirit, a pro-civil rights movement and a feeling of excitement about change and empowerment."

Among the faculty who modeled activism for students, Rick Whitehead took students to antiwar protests both locally and in Washington, D.C. He had come to Windsor Mountain after finishing Brown University in 1967, around the same time as his brother, Peter, was leaving Windsor to attend Brown. During his first semester there, Peter participated in the March on the Pentagon, refused induction into the military, lost his college deferment and spent time in jail, all of which led to a court case that arose because the protestors' deferments were taken away without due process. The case went all the way to the Supreme Court, and Peter and the others made history when they won their case.

"I developed a social conscience at Windsor Mountain," said Caskey Weston, '68. And Ellyn Kravette, '61, now an interfaith minister who works in the corporate mental health field, said, "Windsor gave me a sense of morality and ethics which have defined my life and continue to teach me to this day."

Windsor students were also part of the sizeable audience on October 8, 1969, at the dedication of the W.E.B. Du Bois (1868–1961) home site on Route 23 in Great Barrington, a culmination of a grass-roots effort to have it placed on the National Register of Historic Places. Du Bois, pioneer of the civil rights movement and a founder of the NAACP (National Association for the Advancement of Colored People), was born and grew up in Great Barrington and wrote about his love of the Berkshire Hills and the "golden" river, the Housatonic, which runs through them.[122] A portion of the dedication was posted on YouTube by UMass Amherst's Department of Special Collections and University Archives and titled "Du Bois Homesite Dedication, 1969." The viewer can see Windsor students, among them Beverly Poitier, getting off a school bus, as well as actor Ossie Davis presiding over the event with his wife, actor Ruby Dee, and Julian Bond, then state senator from Georgia, who spoke to the audience about his concerns, still current today, including FBI eavesdropping on citizens' telephone conversations.

It's not surprising that Windsor students attended these events. After all, they represented values like equality, tolerance, peace and justice, which permeated the atmosphere at Windsor Mountain. So it was particularly alarming when, "after MLK's assassination, there was a rift and a separation of races on campus," said Jeannie Whitehead. "African Americans seemed to see all whites as the enemy." Bob Blafield remembered an African American girl who had a stunning voice and was going to join his madrigal group. "Some black students trashed her room because they didn't want her to sing 'whitey music,'" he said. "So she didn't join. The faculty tried to change the self-segregation in the cafeteria but couldn't." "A kind of reverse racism began," said Christopher Smith. "It was the time of the Panthers and Black Power, and Martin Luther King had been assassinated. Blacks were trying to see where they fit in." Pamela Esler remembered that Heinz, in order to help the African American community at Windsor feel empowered, instituted an African American night with food and dancing, to be held whenever the community decided it wanted to organize one.

Despite the fact that some Windsor students participated in the antiwar and civil rights movements, they were, for the most part, indifferent to politics during the first half of the 1970s, according to Lorin Kusmin, '74, now a researcher on rural economic growth for the U.S. Department of Agriculture's Rural Development Agency. He said that he "was one of only a handful of political activists then." Kusmin's activism, however, energized the campus for a while in the fall of 1973, when he initiated a petition that said if Nixon didn't surrender his secret tapes, he should be impeached. It was the time when Nixon was suspected of ordering a cover-up of the Watergate scandal and special prosecutor Archibald Cox was demanding Nixon give up the tapes. The faculty and students all signed Kusmin's petition.

And then there was activism that took the form of eccentric behavior, which might be considered one way of making a political statement. During the late '60s, one eccentric stood out, Larry Abrams, aka Laurence Gilbert Broadmore, '68, who every day dressed like an Edwardian gentleman, replete with gold-tipped cane, gold watch and chain and pince-nez, his message being that nothing created after 1900 is worth wearing, using or advocating.

Alumni remember when Larry figured out how to briefly activate Grenville Winthrop's fountain system by manipulating a water hose in time for the '68 graduation, though it resulted in no more than a trickle. After attending Bard College and living in Tivoli, New York, Abrams became a "painstaking craftsman" repairing and restoring player pianos and "drew customers from all over the state."[123] In 2008, the *Daily News* wrote an article about Larry, now living in California and still restoring player pianos, and noted that his nineteenth-century life lasted nine years, until he turned twenty-five, when, finally, "the stress got to him."[124]

Among other eccentrics, or protestors of a sort, was "a boy who called himself a 'breathatarian,' who believed he could live on air alone and almost starved to death," noted Pamela Esler. She also fondly described her

Larry Abrams, '68, aka Laurence Gilbert Broadmore, in Edwardian clothing. *From 1968 Windsor yearbook.*

somewhat eccentric teacher Oldrich Prochazka, "a real character whom I'll never forget seeing through my window standing naked looking up to the sky in the rain."

THE LID COMES OFF

A faculty member who taught at Windsor in the '70s, who wanted to remain anonymous, responded to my request for an interview with this e-mail:

> *I have been a bit guarded about talking with you about WM because it was truly in demise when I entered the scene. Gertrud was failing, Heinz was distracted, and the place was taking students who were not, as we'd say today, mission appropriate. Strange faculty relationships and hierarchy. It was all very '70s, but without some of the high notes. I'd rather stop at that and let others who experienced the real culture of the school fill you in. I apologize for ducking...*

"Many teachers were demoralized; the place was just unraveling," said Esler about the early '70s. Franny Hall said, "I never wanted to direct any more plays. We weren't getting the same kind of students anymore." Anne Hemenway explained, "There were juvenile court and hospital referrals; it was Windsor Mountain School or jail, the 'last-stop hotel.'" And Anne Klein, who taught history during the last year of the school's life, said there were "delinquents there, unteachables," referring to some wards of the state whom Heinz took in, a decision many believed was not in the best interests of the school or even of the students themselves, who might have benefitted from a more structured and disciplined environment.

Catya von Karolyi, now a professor of psychology at the University of Wisconsin, wrote, "While I loved growing up there [her parents met at Windsor, and her father, "Duck" Daley, taught there], I wasn't comfortable there as a student. During that period, the level of drugs, sex and rock 'n' roll was overwhelming. People were being hospitalized for drug overdoses. My roommate was raped, and my boyfriend became a junkie." Catya left Windsor Mountain after two years for Verde Valley School in Sedona, Arizona.

Windsor wasn't the only school contending with such issues, however. Lorin Kusmin described an assembly held to deal with "an incident" involving a student at another school: "A kid was dealing marijuana, and his supply had been stolen. So he went to get his pot back with some friends. 'We had to defend our turf,' the kid jokingly said. I don't remember all the details." But in fact, the details of that "incident" were reported in the *Berkshire Eagle* on December 6, 1972, in an article titled "Windsor Mt. Student Charged in Stabbing": "Patrick W. James, from Windsor, was charged with stabbing Timothy Pyles in his room at the Stockbridge School. Pyles survived, and James appeared in Lee District Court, his case continued…"

It is important to note, however, that there were several students who, despite this difficult time, experienced what that anonymous teacher called "the real culture of the school," the way it used to be, the way the late Bob Neaman wanted Windsor to be remembered. Charlie Parriott's sister, Susan, explained that her brother stayed out of the drug culture. He went to Windsor because he was a "restless teenager" and about to run away when his parents (the family lived in Lenox) considered Windsor a creative alternative and a way to get him grounded. And "it worked." Charlie became interested in learning Russian and Slavic languages with Jan and Zuzana Wiener, and now he speaks them fluently. However, Charlie said that two of his friends at Windsor overdosed and that he was luckily able to revive them, though "one died a few years later," as did others he knew who were unable to kick their habit.

Kusmin also testified that he personally "did not experience the drug culture" and mentioned several serious students who relished the freedom to pursue their studies and personal interests. One of them, Benjamin Mills, '75, the last valedictorian at Windsor Mountain School and now a doctor, went on to become the Central Asia regional director of the Division of Global HIV/AIDS at the Center for Disease Control and Prevention, among his other important positions in the health field.

"Yes, it was a time of deep confusion in the country—Vietnam, etc.—but Windsor Mountain was like a life raft for many of us," said Gigi Buffington. Echoed Roselle Van Nostrand, "Windsor saved my life. It loved me back to life and pulled the plug on my defensiveness." Roselle had been sent to Windsor Mountain by the State of New Jersey, one of the wards of the state that Heinz accepted "because he needed the money," said several faculty members. (Others, however, said Heinz took in wards of the state because he just wanted to give these kids another chance at life.) Gigi Buffington said, "The wards of the state were as diverse as the students in general. For

Matuschka (Joanne Motichka, '72) on the steps of the Smith House dormitory, 1972. *Courtesy of Jon Frank.*

example, you could be a ward of the state and be a blonde girl whose parents were unable to handle her [Roselle's case], or you could be a troubled kid from Harlem."

Another "blonde girl" who came to Windsor as a ward of New Jersey, Joanne Motichka, '72, now an outstanding artist and photographer, explained how, after her mother died and her father remarried, she ran away from home, got involved with drugs, became a ward of the state and ended up in a series of foster homes until the age of seventeen, when a social worker recommended Windsor Mountain. Once there and living in Smith House, in Lenox, she said, "I got absorbed in my studies in art and photography and completed my high school education."

It was also at Windsor Mountain, she said, "where Gerdi Wiener gave me the name I now use professionally. He yelled out my last name in the

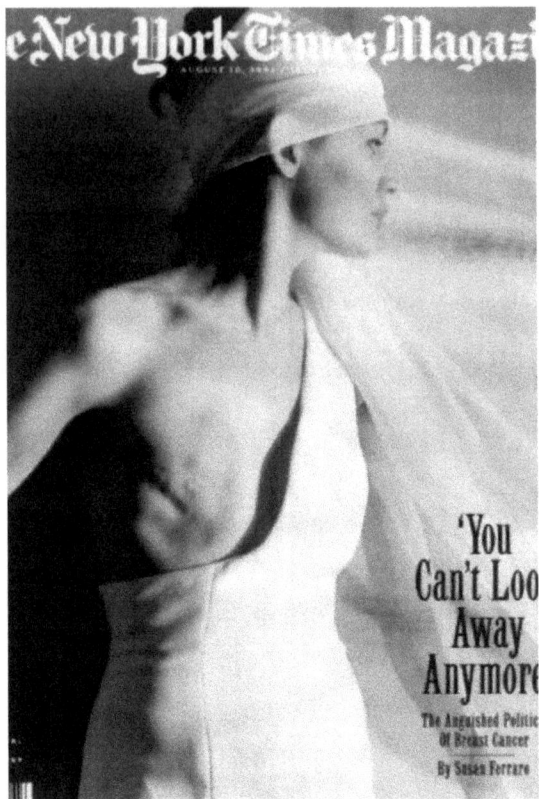

Left: Matuschka on the cover of the August 15, 1993 *New York Times Magazine* in a self-portrait entitled "Beauty Out of Damage." *Courtesy of Matuschka.*

Below: Students Jeffrey Spirer and Betsy Hellman hanging out in class. *From 1969 Windsor yearbook.*

auditorium during roll call: 'MA Tusch KA,' which sounded commanding in his thick accent, much better than Moe-tit-chka." Her fame came later. In 1991, Matuschka had a modified mastectomy, and in August 1993, she bared her mastectomy scar on the cover of the *New York Times Sunday Magazine* in a self-portrait titled "Beauty Out of Damage," which led to international fame and, at the same time, raised awareness of breast cancer.[125]

In a lengthy and very positive article, Stephen C. Rose wrote in the *Berkshire Eagle* on February 4, 1973, about "Windsor Mountain School—Where Students Grow" and quoted Wendell Hale, a graduate who was then serving as a house parent: "I don't see the school as permissive. That has a bad connotation. I see what goes on here as letting people live their own lives as long as they don't hurt others. They might even hurt themselves, and that would be all right if they learned from it."

Was he expressing Heinz's philosophy? Maybe. The kind of laissez-faire policy that Hale describes might have, indeed, worked well for many of Windsor's students, but in the end, it might also have been one of the many factors that led to its demise.

And while there were, indeed, signs in 1974 of Windsor's demise, there were also the words of Alger Hiss, Windsor Mountain's June graduation speaker, who implied that Windsor students could change their world. A Harvard Law School graduate and former U.S. State Department official, Hiss became nationally known in 1948, when he was accused of being part of an alleged communist espionage ring. Citing several episodes in America's history when injustices were committed by government officials, including the McCarthy era and the Watergate scandal, Hiss told the eighty-five graduating seniors that they could help prevent such incidents in the future: "Once people learn to think for themselves, as you have learned to do here, the genie of independent thought cannot be put back in the bottle." Hiss then encouraged students to consider careers in government.[126]

Years before, in 1967, Clifford Durr had conveyed a similar message, in which he told seniors that they were inheriting an imperfect world, but problems wouldn't be solved by those who merely voice objections or seek to find their identities through psychedelics.

Chapter 8

1975–2014: Windsor Mountain School Closes Along with Others; Their Properties Take on New Lives

When I went to visit Windsor Mountain after it closed, the school seemed little changed physically. But it was the end of something so unique and unlike what the world had known or would ever know again.
—Christopher Smith, '70

1975: WINDSOR MOUNTAIN SCHOOL CLOSES

"Windsor Mt. School Closes" was the front-page headline of the *Berkshire Eagle* on August 6, 1975. In this article, Barbara Van Nice wrote: "Bondy said that various efforts are underway and…Windsor Mountain possibly could reorganize and open in 1976." She also mentioned a letter of support from Barbara Tuchman, the prize-winning historian, whose daughter, Alma, had attended Windsor Mountain.

But it was not to be. Windsor had mortgaged the property too many times, and now it could no longer pay its bills or its mortgages. The First Agricultural National Bank of Pittsfield foreclosed on the property. An October article in the *Eagle*, "Windsor Mt. Property to be Auctioned October 22," noted that Windsor's land was assessed for town records at $280,000 and its buildings for $1.5 million and that Heinz Bondy was living in the Boston area and working as a consultant for Stockbridge School.

The extent of any reorganization efforts at the time is unclear, but Tom Roeper, grandson of the Bondys, wrote, "Before the school closed, an effort was made to raise money to save it. I and my father [George Roeper] sought to raise $20,000 from family members. I gave $2,000 myself (not so easy for a new assistant prof)…" He noted that when the school was finally liquidated, he and his parents had some small claim on the proceeds. His father had originally had a 15 percent share in the school "because he had a little inheritance and used some of it to buy the school originally." A November 5, 1975 *Berkshire Eagle* article, "Holliston Jr. College Offers $350,000 for Windsor Mt. Site," referred to George A. and Thomas Roeper and their concern about retrieving their money from the foreclosure sale of the school. "I cannot remember if we got a few hundred back," wrote Tom. The final sale of the school to Holliston Junior College was confirmed in the *Berkshire Eagle* on December 18, 1975, in an article titled "Holliston Takes Title to Lenox Site." The college paid the bank $270,000.[127]

So why did Windsor Mountain School close? First of all, there were economic and social factors that affected not only Windsor Mountain but also eight other private preparatory Berkshire boarding schools that closed around the same time. There were also causes specific to Windsor Mountain.

In terms of the economic situation, the United States was suffering from a recession in the 1970s that led to financial woes for many of these boarding schools and to a decline in enrollments and donations, along with escalating costs.[128] With the 1973–74 stock market crash and the 1973 oil embargo, which caused the price of oil to skyrocket, the cost of heating the old mansions that these schools inhabited became prohibitive. Richard Neely wrote about some of these issues on the school's website on February 14, 2007:

> *What had happened is that the entire market for private secondary education had changed by 1972. A combination of an inter-generational leveling in the distribution of wealth, i.e., younger parents didn't have the spare money that their parents had had to afford private school,* together with changes in social attitudes, limited the market for paying students. [Along with the 1960s revolutions in sex, drugs, students' rights, civil rights and gender], *there were the anti-establishment, anti-elitist attitudes that caused younger parents to disparage private schooling as "elitist."*

In terms of the causes specific to Windsor Mountain's closing, Neely's assessment is worth serious attention because he was not only a graduate of the school and a lawyer but also a member of Windsor's board in 1974. "I participated to a larger extent than most in trying to save the school," he wrote. "I traveled from West Virginia to the school in Lenox once a month for about a year to try and keep the school from closing." Neely went on:

In the last years we continued to get a lot of really interesting, motivated, agreeable students, but our problem was that in order to pay the bills, including some horrific mortgages incurred to build the new boys' and girls' dorms and the theater, we needed to take more and more students sponsored by the State of Massachusetts [Department of Youth Services] *and the State of Rhode Island. Some of these students were simply orphans or neglected children, but others came from the juvenile justice system and were definitely not Windsor material.*

Even the students who had no delinquency problems did not come with the depth of background our earlier students possessed. The influx of state-sponsored students, plus lowering of standards, came very close to destroying the atmosphere of the school. So at the time the school closed, there was extremely low faculty and administration morale, partially, of course, because faculty and administration knew we were hanging on by our fingernails. For example, the school began to suffer deliberate vandalism of the buildings, something unheard of in my day as a student. Oddly enough, the old Saturday Review of Literature *did a feature story on WMS and allowed as to how WMS did a much better job with keeping drug usage down than any of the other prep schools, notwithstanding the unstructured façade. But it wasn't enough. With the change in the nature of the students, it was not possible to run Windsor in the way Windsor was traditionally run.*

Echoed Terry Hall, "The school was all about giving students freedom. And these students—some of whom had committed crimes—they needed more structure. The school was not meant to be a reform school." (Heinz might have benefitted from the expertise of his uncle Curt Bondy, whose research was related to bringing juvenile delinquents back into society.) And Jeannie Whitehead wondered if it had been a good idea for Heinz to give so many scholarships. Taking in scholarship students had always been a part of the Bondy philosophy, and every year more than 15 percent of the students didn't pay tuition. (Nearly every student I interviewed had been on a full or partial scholarship.)

Maurice Eldridge, assistant headmaster at Windsor from 1967 to 1975, is currently vice-president of college/community relations and executive assistant to the president at Swarthmore College. *Courtesy of Swarthmore College.*

Pamela Esler offered a different perspective: "Heinz let the school self-destruct. He didn't want to be there in the first place, but he felt duty-bound. He didn't have to let things go, but he wanted to on some level." She referred to the fact that the school closed at the same time that Carolyn, his wife, was about to go to medical school in Boston, and "he wanted to join her." Faculty member Franny Hall agreed, saying that she and Jim, and others, including assistant headmaster Maurice Eldridge, believed they could have salvaged the situation—"maybe cut salaries, try different things"—had they been warned about the imminent closing. But one student close to Heinz said in his defense, "Heinz had not given any indication earlier that the school was in danger of closing, because he didn't want to take the chance that the graduating class would be at risk of not getting to finish the school year."

Eldridge, who had himself participated in fundraising efforts all along, was "shocked" and experienced "grief" and a "feeling of betrayal" when the end came. It was, he said, "not the kind of openness we were used to." He and some of the other faculty were not only left without a job but also had mortgages to deal with. Whether or not these faculty members could have made it work will never be known, but they wished they had had a chance to find out, despite what looked like an impossible financial situation.[129]

Bill Dobbs offered still other contributing factors that might have led to the inevitable: "When a school has been established by a charismatic leader like Gertrud—with a reputation for compassion and an early association with Freud—a cult of personality may develop," noted Dobbs, "and it's difficult for anyone else to take their place." And he added, "Society may simply have caught up with Windsor Mountain." The school had been ahead of its time in terms of integration, liberation and student empowerment, but with the arrival of the '60s civil rights laws, the eighteen-year-old vote and "diversity" becoming the buzzword in public schools, "Windsor Mountain was no longer the radical alternative it had once been."

Whatever the combination of reasons for Windsor's closing, "The ending was abrasive to say the least, and the faculty felt slighted," said Franny Hall. Richard Neely concluded with this observation, which alumni may or may not agree with: "The bottom line is that Windsor, circa 1972 to 1975 [the 'dark years,' he called them] was not the Windsor that we all knew from 1948 to 1965. There was still a core of the old Windsor-type students, but there weren't enough of them to sustain a critical mass, which is probably why we found our market for paying students dwindling. It was a vicious cycle."

Windsor's very last graduation ceremony, June 1975, was the subject of a *Berkshire Eagle* article on June 9, 1975, "Windsor Mountain Graduates 70." The article noted that Stephan Ross, then forty-four, one of the Holocaust survivors Max and Gertrud had taken in after the war, was the graduation speaker.

And just weeks before the school officially closed, an *Eagle* article on July 17, 1975, "Windsor Mt. to Continue if Enough Pupils Enroll," published Heinz's response to a question about Windsor's closing:

> *"I can't guarantee we'll open, but we're certainly trying."* Bondy did say, *however, that a final decision would be made by the school's board of trustees. Reports of trouble at Windsor Mountain intensified this week after a meeting Tuesday of Bondy,* the school's lawyer [Frederick M. Myers Jr. of the Pittsfield firm of Cain, Hibbard and Myers] *and a bank official.*

Windsor's board of trustees did, indeed, make the final decision and officially closed the school on August 6, 1975.

1970–80: OTHER SCHOOLS CLOSE

Windsor Mountain was not the only secondary private boarding school to close between 1970 and 1980. Excluding the therapeutic boarding schools in the area, eight other mostly well-established and prestigious boarding schools in the Berkshires and environs closed around the same time. (Most, like Windsor Mountain, had taken up residence in the 1940s in one of the Berkshires' Gilded Age summer "cottages," vacated by families whose wealth and buying power had diminished as a result of the income tax law, the Great Depression and the effects of World War II.[130] The properties had become affordable, and educators, enamored of these gorgeous, expansive environments, stepped in to take advantage of them as boarding schools.)

Barlow School (1940–80), in nearby Amenia, New York, in "the foothills of the Berkshires"[131] was, like Windsor Mountain, a progressive school and counted among its graduates men and women who went on to careers in the arts, among them actor Chris Noth. Kildonan School, a boarding and day school for students with dyslexia, now owns the former Barlow site.

Stockbridge School (1949–76), again, like Windsor, a progressive boarding school, closed soon after Windsor Mountain. Located in the Interlaken section of Stockbridge, Massachusetts, the campus eventually became the site of DeSisto School (1978–2004), a controversial, private, therapeutic boarding school for troubled teens. The property currently stands vacant.

Also closing during the 1970s was Cornwall Academy for Boys (1951–74), founded by John Geddes Moran, in the south Berkshire town of Great Barrington. Poet Michael Houlihan, who came to the school in the '60s to teach languages and history, said that Windsor was looked upon as "avant-garde, not of the mold of most private schools. And though I saw Windsor kids 'under the influence,' kids at Cornwall—with its veneer of discipline—would do the same things!" Private homes and condominiums now occupy the former Cornwall campus.

The other five schools that closed were, like Windsor, located in Lenox. The one with the longest history, Lenox School for Boys (1926–72)—founded by Episcopal churchmen but nondenominational—was, like Windsor, proud of its early focus on diversity and service to others.[132] When Lenox School merged with the Bordentown Military Institute, a private high school in Bordentown, New Jersey (1881–1973), in 1972, it became known as the Bordentown-Lenox School, but the combined entity closed after one year.[133] Mark Selkowitz, president of the Mark Selkowitz Insurance Agency in Pittsfield, Massachusetts, a graduate and chair of the school's board of trustees when it closed, shared the fact that "the school had just built a huge recreation center that someone had said they would pay for but, in the end, didn't come up with the money. So we couldn't pay for the new building or anything else." (A story similar to the one about Windsor's new theater that Max Jacobson was going to fund but never did.) The main parcel occupied by Lenox School is now the home of Shakespeare and Company. The Kemble Inn sits on another parcel, adjacent to several smaller private properties.

Cranwell School (1939–75), established by the Society of Jesus (Jesuits), was another Lenox boarding school that closed in the '70s. James Gill, a ninth-grade student in 1945, described the school in a memoir, noting that Teddy Kennedy, the late senator from Massachusetts, had been in the eighth grade there.[134] The school had taken over an estate built by Reverend Ward Beecher, brother of Harriet Beecher Stowe, and the grounds were designed by Frederick Law Olmstead, responsible for New York City's Central Park. Cranwell Resort, Spa and Golf Club now occupies the property. In recalling the years he was a day student at Cranwell from 1963 to '67, Terry Flynn, a retired teacher, wrote:

> My sense is that Cranwell was perceived as a place of solid values…while WM was seen as wild and loose, influenced by the beat generation. But I doubt very much if either picture was accurate. Cranwell had many troubled students, and neither its education nor its discipline were superior to Williams High School [the local public high school] in Stockbridge.

Rockwood Academy (1964–75) closed the same year as Windsor Mountain and Cranwell. Richard J. Herbert Jr. had purchased the former Overleigh estate in 1964 and, like Heinz Bondy, tried to stay afloat by taking in wards of the state from the Department of Youth Services. But problems arose, as they did at Windsor Mountain, and Rockwood closed because of lack of funds. Herbert sold the property in 1980 to Hillcrest Education Centers, a private nonprofit agency that continues to operate a network of campuses in Lenox, Great Barrington and Pittsfield for students with behavioral difficulties.

Foxhollow School for Girls, founded in 1898, in the Hudson River area, moved to Lenox in 1939 to an estate originally owned by inventor and industrialist George Westinghouse. It was later purchased by Margaret Emerson McKim Vanderbilt Baker Amory Emerson, who eventually sold it in 1939 to Aileen M. Farrell, who operated Foxhollow until 1976. Today, it is a condominium resort known as The Ponds at Foxhollow.[135] Interestingly, in the 1950s, when Farrell wanted to expand her school, she purchased the Mount, the estate of author Edith Wharton, to use as a girls' dormitory. Wharton's estate, including the house and gardens, has since been restored and designated a U.S. National Historic Landmark and operates today as a center for cultural activities celebrating the literary arts and Wharton's achievements.

The last school in Lenox to close during the economic downturn was the Immaculate Heart of Mary Seminary (1961–79), run by the Priests of the Sacred Heart as a school for young men interested in the priesthood. It was once the site of the summer "cottage," Bellefontaine, and since 1987 has been occupied by Canyon Ranch, a health and wellness resort known for catering to celebrities and the wealthy.[136]

However, a handful of college preparatory boarding schools in the Berkshires (not counting schools designated for students with behavioral or learning differences) survived the economic and social problems of the '70s. Unlike those that closed, these schools might have had substantial endowments, alumni associations and/or large contributors to keep them going. And all of them could claim deeper roots in the area. They include Buxton School (1928), in Williamstown; Berkshire School (1907), in Sheffield; Miss Hall's School (1898), in Pittsfield; and three schools that identify their locations as in or near the Berkshire Hills: Darrow School (1932), in New Lebanon, New York; Hotchkiss School (1891), in Lakeville, Connecticut; and Salisbury School (1901), in Salisbury, Connecticut.

Commenting on the presence of so many private boarding schools in the Berkshires in general and in Lenox in particular, historian David Wood wrote, "The impact that public and private schools collectively have had on the atmosphere of Berkshire is incalculable, but it undoubtedly accounts for the fact that instinctively talent and culture feel at home in these hills."[137]

Stockbridge School, Windsor Mountain's Neighbor

Worthy of further discussion is Stockbridge School because of its similarities to Windsor Mountain. Both schools attracted students who, for one reason or another, did not see themselves fitting into a more traditional setting, public or private. One of Stockbridge School's most famous alumni from the '60s, folksinger and musician Arlo Guthrie, starred in the film *Alice's Restaurant*, about which he also wrote a twenty-minute song that captures scenes of the Berkshires—including a memorable Thanksgiving celebration. The "Alice" of the song and film, Alice Brock, former librarian at Stockbridge School when Arlo was a student, later opened a lunch counter in the town. Guthrie currently lives in Washington, Berkshire County, Massachusetts, and presides over the nonprofit Guthrie Center and Foundation, out of the former "Alice's Church" (the Old Trinity Church) in the Van Deusenville section of Great Barrington, and is dedicated to "working together with other non-profit agencies to serve those in need," the kind of mission the founders of both schools would have supported.[138] Arlo responded to a question about connections between the two schools:

> We used to play soccer against them, and I visited the school for dances and social activities. Their headmaster [Heinz] had at one time worked with Hans Maeder [founder and headmaster of Stockbridge School] and maybe had a falling out, but not enough of one to stop the social lines of communication from being open between students. The Windsor Mountain philosophy was similar at least as far as dress codes [there were none at that time] and things of that nature. Hans and Ruth Maeder and the staff of Stockbridge School had some kind of reasonable relationship with Windsor staff, but I was really out of that loop.

Barbara Cohen-Hobbs, a classmate of Arlo's, said, "There was a rivalry between the two schools. There was Hans and Heinz, both German, both with war experiences. The kids from the two schools would get together and smoke pot and have a blast." Sometimes they would meet up on weekends at Mundy's Bar and Restaurant (1970–89), located in the Glendale section of Stockbridge, "a hangout for hippies, bikers, artists and local politicians," said Billy Kie, a local man of all trades who used to hang out there with Windsor Mountain and Stockbridge School students and faculty. "The bar was run by Fred Mundy, a worldly guy who went to Brown [University], a real raconteur."

According to research by James Cass, Hans Maeder (1909–1988) was born in Hamburg and was a refugee like the Bondys, though he wasn't Jewish. Having participated in the anti-Nazi underground, he fled Germany in 1933 to avoid arrest. When Max and Gertrud invited him to join the faculty at the Windsor Mountain School in 1944 (Maeder had been familiar with the Bondys' school in Germany), he accepted and taught at Windsor for a year, after which he taught and served as director at the Walden School, a progressive private school in New York City.[139]

Wanting to start his own school, Maeder purchased the Hanna estate in 1947. And by 1949, he opened Stockbridge School, where he established most of the practices he had observed while at Windsor Mountain School, among them co-education; student-centered, hands-on learning; morning music before classes; student participation in dining room duties; calling teachers by their first names; extensive student government; jackets and ties for boys and dresses for girls at dinner (in the early years); respect for differences and for social justice on a diverse and international campus (the flag of the United Nations flew at Stockbridge School); and a dual concern for individual rights and the welfare of the community.

In addition, both Hans and Heinz believed in offering generous scholarships to inner-city youth, refugees and children from local families. Like the Bondys, Maeder hired a diverse faculty, and when Windsor Mountain closed in August 1975, the headmaster at Stockbridge School (Maeder had already left by then) invited Windsor faculty and students to come to Stockbridge. Several accepted the offer, but in 1976, Stockbridge School, too, closed, unable to finish out that school year.

Ben Barber, a 1956 graduate of Stockbridge School and now a renowned political scientist, was devoted to the school's vision and considered the place a nurturing environment, adding that "for some like me, it was a first home."[140] "Ninety percent of the kids at Stockbridge were there because their parents wanted to unload them somewhere. Either they had problems, or their parents had problems, or their parents just wanted to get them out of their hair," wrote Barber. (For example, both parents of Chevy Chase, another famous graduate of Stockbridge School, had had multiple divorces. And Jackie Robinson Jr.'s parents had heard that the school could help him with his emotional problems.)

Would Windsor Mountain alumni (and Stockbridge alumni) identify with the way in which Barber characterized them? While some might view the figure of "ninety percent" as an exaggeration, it is likely that a great number of Windsor students would agree with him, considering their testimony during our interviews. Nevertheless, whatever problems some of these students came in with, "by the time they were ready to graduate," said Franny Hall, "we could see how they had found themselves or found love or something." And, said teacher Haldor Reinholt, "Basically most came out of Windsor happier than when they came in." Both schools had tried to address the needs of every one of their students by giving them a chance to "be who they are," and more often than not, they succeeded, according to those who continue to say, "That school saved my life."

1975–2014: USES OF THE CAMPUS AFTER WINDSOR MOUNTAIN'S CLOSING

A November 5, 1975 article in the *Berkshire Eagle* announced the following: "Holliston Jr. College, located south of Framingham, MA, is considering the Windsor Mountain site as an addition to its present campus for training of paramedics, medical assistants, veterinary assistants, respiratory therapists and food technologists."[141]

A month or so later, Holliston did, in fact, purchase the property for $270,000. It wasn't long after that that Ann Getsinger, a Berkshire artist, took up residence in a tiny room in the stone mansion at the former Windsor property, staying there for about a year between the time that Windsor Mountain closed and when Beatrice Macmunn, the owner of Holliston Junior College, opened the Berkshire branch of her college. Getsinger explained that Macmunn rented out a few rooms at first and then several more, adding that she also allowed a service dog program to use the campus. The Hearing Ear Dog Program, begun in 1976, involved teaching dogs to read hand signals, but the program didn't last long. And because Holliston never received accreditation, Macmunn ended up selling off several parcels of the property. (It is ironic that the former Windsor site was used for dog training, since there were always "packs of dogs"—some not so well trained—running around the school, according to Eric Bondy.)

Getsinger remembered Macmunn as a kind and generous person who lived in an apartment on one end of the second floor, likely the one in which Gertrud Bondy had lived. Ann said she didn't know anything about Windsor Mountain but had heard that "the kids were always high," a description that apparently still applied, because, she said, "There was still a lot of pot around the building." Ann described her time there as "laid-back and easygoing; one guy raised chickens in his room, and an assortment of male renters would get together and smoke and philosophize."

Then one day, she said, there was "a sudden change in atmosphere" in what appeared to be "an overnight deal." Nick Thaw, who was renting out the theater on campus, had invited Ann to live temporarily in the space under the back of the stage once the Holliston program began. She said, "I remember waking up one morning and hearing someone greeting people with a rather Bible-rousing, Jesus-loving kind of talk. The campus took on a militaristic air with people driving around every night with searchlights." It turned out that Macmunn had rented out the campus to the Stevens School of the Bible, also known as "The Bible Speaks West." The non-accredited college was the creation of Pastor Carl H. Stevens, who rented the Holliston (Windsor) campus from 1976 until 1980, when the site was sold to Boston University.[142]

CONCLUSION

In the summer of 1963, Boston University began renting space from Windsor Mountain School. And in 1967, the university's College of Fine Arts' School of Music began operating a summer music school—the Boston University Tanglewood Institute (BUTI)—for gifted high school–age musicians. The program was the "brainchild of then Boston Symphony's music director, Erich Leinsdorf, who sought a high school level program to complement the orchestra's institute [the Tanglewood Music Center] for

Students at the Boston University Tanglewood Institute playing music on the lawn at Tanglewood. *Courtesy of the Berkshire Eagle, Pittsfield, MA.*

Scenic Berkshire view on the Windsor campus. *From 1969 Windsor yearbook.*

college-age and advanced professionals," wrote Clarence Fanto in an *Eagle* article on October 8, 2013, titled "BU Program Will Return for 2014." The university finally purchased the sixty-four-acre, former Windsor Mountain property for $590,000 in 1980 (when Holliston Junior College went bankrupt).[143]

In that same article, Brenda Patterson, who attended the Boston University Tanglewood Institute's program in 1994 and 1995, said the following: "I speak for many of us when I say that the BUTI grounds are a sacred space to us, a place of peace, discovery, and creativity. [It] is the place from which all my inspiration springs, an experience that is not replicable just anywhere." Interestingly, Windsor Mountain students say much the same thing about their beloved school.

Epilogue: The Bondy Legacy Continues

*In the scheme of life, the existence of the Windsor/Bondy experiment as a
formula for improving the human condition was less than a hiccup, yet it affected
dramatically the lives of multiple generations.*
—Christopher Smith, '70

Alumni gathered in the hundreds for a reunion on the site of their beloved school in Lenox in 1996 and again in somewhat smaller numbers in 2006. And all around the country, mini reunions are held, some as often as every year, so that alumni can embrace and share stories that remind them of how lucky they were to have been part of the Bondy experiment in the midst of the idyllic Berkshire Hills.

Judy Levin, who became a social worker, described how each attendee at the '96 reunion stood up—many in tears that also rippled through the audience—and spoke about what Windsor meant to them and how Windsor had influenced who and what they became, many mentioning their work in the helping professions and the arts. Their words reverberated years later in the remarks that Maurice Eldridge made at Heinz Bondy's memorial service in April 2014. Said Eldridge, "Graduates of Windsor Mountain School are like seeds cast to the winds that spread the spirit and values of Windsor throughout their own lives and the lives of those they touch."

The Bondys' legacy also continues to thrive at two schools: Schule Marienau, in Germany, Max and Gertrud's first school, and The Roeper

Schule Marienau. *Courtesy of Schule Marienau and the Roeper family.*

The Roeper School. *Courtesy of Roeper School Archives.*

School (their "first daughter school," said Gertrud), founded in 1941 by Max and Gertrud's daughter, Annemarie, and her husband, George Roeper. Marienau's history—as the creation of German Jews—was largely forgotten until 1989, when then-headmaster Wolf-Dieter Hasenclever created the Bondy Haus as a repository for the Bondy-Roeper archives and merged the Bondy philosophy and the ideals of the youth movement with his philosophy of ecological humanism that still prevails there and likely accounts for Marienau, in 2003, becoming a UNESCO project school "committed to human rights, peaceful international understanding, environmental education and intercultural learning."

The Roeper School, located in Bloomfield Hills and Birmingham, Michigan, operates today as a private day school "where gifted students love to learn" and in many ways replicates the mission of Annemarie's parents. The school's homepage notes that Roeper alumni "can be found throughout the world building on the creativity, critical thinking, and collaborative skills" that they learned there.

Windsor alumni, together with graduates of Schule Marienau and The Roeper School, both fruits of the Bondy legacy, remain living examples of how—despite two world wars and the Nazi Holocaust—beauty, love and human goodness can and does survive.

Notes

Preface

1. Robert U. Johnson, "Windsor Mt. School Opens with 118 Boys, Girls Enrolled," *Berkshire Eagle*, September 19, 1955, 20.
2. Katie Zeima, "Opposition to Standardized Tests Grows," *Berkshire Eagle*, September 9, 2013, 1–2; *New York Times*, "Standing Up to Testing," March 30, 2014, 1, 5.

Chapter 1

3. *Dictionary of American Family Names.*
4. Cramer, "In Memory of the Bondys." Ernst Cramer (1913–2010) was a prize-winning German Jewish journalist and playwright who, as a young man, assisted Max Bondy's brother, Curt, at the agricultural training camp at Gross Breesen and later became a lifelong friend of Max and Gertrud's.
5. Roeper and Mireau, *Marienau*, 30.
6. Ibid., 31.
7. Ibid., 45–46.
8. Ibid., 84.
9. Ibid., 160.

10. Ibid., 159.

11. Gorres, *Broken Lights*.

12. Roeper and Mireau, *Marienau*, 85.

13. Walter Laqueur, "The German Youth Movement," 79–83, 198. (Max Bondy's quote originally appeared in *Friedeutsche Jugend*, 1916, 322.)

14. Roeper and Mireau, *Marienau*, 88.

15. Mendes-Flohr and Reinharz, *Jew in the Modern World*, 312.

16. Roeper and Mireau, *Marienau*, 97.

17. Ibid., 123.

18. Ibid., 167.

19. Ibid., 119, 189–90.

20. Ursula "Ulla" Bondy (1921–1970), Max and Gertrud's younger daughter, was a psychiatric social worker. Married to Dr. Donald Gerard, a psychiatrist, she had three children, one of whom, Kathleen "Kay" Gerard Whitney, an artist, attended Windsor Mountain as a tenth grader briefly in 1964.

21. Kersken, *Report*.

22. Roeper and Mireau, *Marienau*, 12.

23. In 1965, students at Windsor Mountain School gave Gertrud a compilation of speeches that she and Max had given to students over the years. Gertrud's analysis of the causes of prejudice—insecurity, fear, anxiety, anger, aggression and ignorance—reveal her insights into the psychology of human behavior and humanism. The compilation is available on the Windsor Mountain School Reunion website, posted by former student Betsy Ryan in January 2014.

24. Roeper and Mireau, *Marienau*, 142.

25. Catalina Gaitan, "Anti-Semitic Incidents Rose in Mass in 2013, Report Says," *Boston Globe*, April 1, 2014.

26. Roeper and Mireau, *Marienau*, 91.

27. Ibid., 113.

28. Ibid., 166–67.

29. Ibid., 167–68.

30. Kane, "Conversation with Annemarie Roeper."

31. Roeper and Mireau, *Marienau*, 170.

32. On August 30, 2012, Heinz told the story of his life and his war experiences to an interviewer from the United States Holocaust Memorial Museum. The recording can be accessed at: www.collections.ushmm.org/search/…irn4782.

33. Peter Whitehead has built homes in the Berkshires for, among others, James Taylor, Yo Yo Ma and Governor Deval Patrick.

34. Gross Breesen is a small village in Silesia, now mostly situated in Poland. The farm school was established on an estate that encompassed farmland, several buildings and a large manor house.

35. Angress, *Between Fear and Hope*, 43–45. The agency that Leo Baeck headed, the National Representative Agency for German Jews, was disbanded during the pogrom Kristallnacht or "Night of Broken Glass," on November 9, 1938, when Nazis burned synagogues and Jewish businesses and arrested thirty thousand Jewish men in Germany.

36. Ibid., 44–46.

37. Ibid., 48.

38. Ibid., 60.

39. Ibid., 67–75.

40. Cramer, "In Memory of the Bondys."

41. Roeper and Mireau, *Marienau*, 62.

42. Ibid., 60.

43. Cat Contiguglia, "Jan Wiener Dies at Age 90," *Prague Post*, December 1, 2010.

44. Gerry Hausman, "Jan Wiener, My Friend," in Wiener, *Assassination of Heydrich*, 168.

45. Wiener, *Assassination of Heydrich*, 162.

46. Ibid., 161; Jan Wiener, "Conversations," WAMC Northeast Public Radio, 2008; Roeper and Mireau, *Marienau*, 185.

47. In his Northeast Public Radio interview, Jan refers to a letter he received from Eleanor Roosevelt in 1959, in which she said: "Your aunt [Gertrud] asked me to write to you…" Roosevelt tells Jan to ask the authorities in Prague for a passport and to show them her letter inviting him to America. Jan was then granted permission to leave temporarily.
Sarah Malcolm, FDR Library archivist, also described a letter to Mrs. Roosevelt, dated March 28, 1961, in which Heinz Bondy invited her to give the graduation address at Windsor Mountain. A notation from Mrs. Roosevelt on the letter states, "'Regret' making no more engagements for June."

48. Shari Rudavsky, "Thomas G. Winner, Scholar, Escaped Nazi Oppression," *Boston Globe*, May 1, 2004.

Chapter 2

49. Max Bondy, 1937 address to the Marienauer Conference.
50. Roeper and Mireau, *Marienau*, 36.
51. Ibid., 38–39.
52. Cramer, "In Memory of the Bondys."
53. Laqueur, "German Youth Movement," 203.
54. Roeper and Mireau, *Marienau*, 85.
55. Laqueur, *Young Germany*, 4–7; Gorres, *Broken Lights*. The Wandervogel (1896–1919) was only the first phase of the youth movement. Several post–World War I phases included branches that fell all across the political spectrum.
56. Dennis Shirley, *Politics of Progressive Education*; Veevers and Allison, *Kurt Hahn*.
57. Lamberti, "Radical School Teachers," 24.
58. Ibid., 35–36; Chartock, *Educational Foundations*, 119–23, 143–49; Roeper and Mireau, *Marienau*, 91.
59. Rockefeller, *John Dewey*, 17.
60. Roeper and Mireau, *Marienau*, 41, 63–81.
61. Kater, *Different Drummers*, 105–08.
62. Roeper and Mireau, *Marienau*, 67.
63. Ibid., 93.
64. Ibid., 94.
65. Ibid., 96–97; *Across Time and Space*.
66. Roeper and Mireau, *Marienau*, 112.
67. Ibid., 112, 189.
68. Ibid., 189.
69. Harald Baruschke, a former student at Schule Marienau and friend of George Roeper's there, married Hannele, a friend of Annemarie Bondy's, at Marienau. Their son, Peter, '56, and two daughters, Barbara, '60, and Christiane, '63, all attended Windsor Mountain School, and both women married men they met at Windsor, respectively, Bob McCormick, '57, and the late Bob Neaman, '62. Michael Baruschke, another son, went to Japan, where Harald had a company that made type in all languages. He got in touch with one of Windsor's only Japanese students, Kensuke Watanaba, and ended up marrying Kensuke's sister.
70. Roeper and Mireau, *Marienau*, 114.
71. Cathy Hoyt of the Windsor (VT) Historical Society found this article.

Chapter 3

72. Prior to meeting the Bondys, Churchill had rented out his mansion a few miles from Windsor, Vermont, for three summers (1915–18) to President Woodrow Wilson for use as his "Summer Capital." (Janice Brown, "The American Winston Churchill (1871–1947)," Cow Hampshire Blog, February 16, 2008, www.cowhampshireblog.com.)

73. The *Thousander*, "In Memoriam: Ann (Mackinnon) Kucera Obituary," November 2009. The *Thousander* is the newsletter of the International Society for Philosophical Inquiry, www.thethousand.com.

74. Faas with Trombacco, *Robert Creeley*, 32.

75. Ibid., 334.

76. Ibid., 334–35.

77. Ibid., 335.

78. The *Guardian*, "Obituary: Hugo Moser," February 20, 2007.

79. Robert Bruce, "Grenville Lindall Winthrop (1864–1943)," http://www.findagrave.com/cgi-bin/fg.cgi?page=gr&GRid=8876342 (Winthrop is buried in the historic Green-Wood Cemetery in Brooklyn, New York); Christopher Reed, "Grenville Lindall Winthrop," http://harvardmagazine.com/2003/03/unveiled.html; Wexler, *Reared in a Greenhouse*, 230.

80. Wexler, *Reared in a Greenhouse*, 230–31.

81. Ibid., 226. Ethylwynde, the Lenox estate of Grenville's mother, is now an event space owned by Jamie and Ethan Berg.

82. Imogene Stanley, "Father's Fears Immured Girls," *Los Angeles Times*, September 11, 1924.

83. "Winthrop Sisters..." *New York Times*, September 7, 1924. Reproductions of the articles related to the scandal that appeared in major newspapers around the country were provided by Bill Dobbs.

84. Black Mountain College, "Cynthia Homire: Vision Quest," http://www.blackmountaincollege.org/news/pressrelease/316-cynthia-homire-vision-quest-press-release.

85. Black Mountain College had been a magnet for budding artists and renowned teachers, among them choreographer Merce Cunningham, lifelong friend and early roommate of Franny Hall's; artists Willem de Kooning and Josef Albers; Bauhaus architect Walter Gropius; composer John Cage; artist Franz Kline; and poet Robert Creeley. Artist Robert Rauschenberg was a student there, as was film director Arthur Penn, who years later had a home in the Berkshires.

Chapter 4

86. Katie Zeima, "Opposition to Standardized Tests Grows," *Berkshire Eagle*, September 9, 2013, 1, 2; *New York Times*, "Standing Up to Testing," March 30, 2014, 1, 5.
87. Gialuco, "My Educational Experiences."

Chapter 5

88. Herb Denton Sr. was principal of an elementary school that was closed by Governor Orval Faubus during the desegregation crisis of 1958, when President Dwight D. Eisenhower sent in troops to enforce the *Brown v. Board of Education* decision outlawing segregation. Herbert Jr., who died in 1989 at the age of forty-five, was a graduate of Harvard and one of the first blacks to reach a position of authority at the *Washington Post*. (*New York Times*, "Herbert Denton, 45, Foreign Correspondent," May 2, 1989.)
89. Arthur Myers, "Toward Adjustment, Away from Conformity," *Berkshire Eagle*, February 15, 1963, 20.
90. *Los Angeles Times*, "Jean Wilkinson Dies at 96; One of the first Los Angeles Teachers to be Fired During Red Scare," January 6, 2011.
91. Barnard, *Outside the Magic Circle*, 292. The Regal Café case involved a group of white students who came to Montgomery to find out more about the treatment of the local black population. They went into an African American café to talk with black students and were arrested for provoking a breach of the peace.
92. Dreier, *100 Greatest Americans*.
93. Barnard, *Outside the Magic Circle*, 255–66; Dorothy Zellner, "Virginia Durr and Rosa Parks, Heroines of the Civil Rights Movement," *Jewish Currents* (May 2006).
94. Eldridge, Baccalaureate Address.
95. *Berkshire Eagle*, "7 Birmingham Negroes to Attend Windsor Mountain School in Lenox," May 4, 1964.
96. Wendover's Dairy Bar on Church Street included the following phrase in its ad in the '57 yearbook: "Windsor's second dining room." Other ads revealed some of the places frequented by Windsor students, like the Friendly's in Lee and Coakley's News Room at the town hall in Lenox.

97. *Berkshire Eagle*, "Empty Dormitory Destroyed by $50,000 Blaze in Lenox," September 3, 1958.

98. Ibid., "$40,000 Dining Hall Built at Windsor Mountain School," June 11, 1960.

Chapter 6

99. A documentary about the Music Inn and School of Jazz was made in 2005, and a website describes their history: www.musicinn.org/history-of-the-music-inn. Jeremy Yudkin's book *The Lenox School of Jazz* tells the story of the school. The inn closed in 1979, and David Rothstein, its third owner, developed condominiums on the site. The School of Jazz was situated in a nearby summer "cottage" that the Barbers had bought called Wheatleigh, which is now an upscale inn. Randy Weston, in his autobiography, *African Rhythms,* recounts how he came to play for ten summers at Berkshire resorts. "The Berkshires [opened] up a whole new world to me," he wrote, and they inspired his "Berkshire Blues."

100. Kelley, *Thelonius Monk,* 387.

101. Belafonte and Schnayerson, *My Song,* 240.

102. Ibid., 368.

103. Ibid., 411.

104. Ibid., 368, 410.

105. Author's Den, http://www.authorsden.com/visit/author, January 11, 2010.

106. Hugh H. and Mabel M. Smythe Papers, www.hdl.loc.gov/loc.mss/eadmss.ms001042.3.

107. Cohodas, *Queen,* 435.

108. Ibid., 448.

109. Leroy Watson Jr., "Forgotten Stories of Courage and Inspiration: Roy Campanella," Bleacher Report, May 1, http://bleacherreport.com/articles/166177-forgotten-stories-of-courage-and-inspiration-roy-campanella.

110. *New York Times,* "Russell D. Hemenway," February 2, 2014, 23.

111. Michael McAuliffe, "Mass Residents Find Way to D.C.," *Republican Newsroom,* November 30, 2008.

112. Judy Collins, *Sweet Judy Blue Eyes,* 296.

113. Ibid., *Singing Lessons,* 188.

Chapter 7

114. Nachman/Dykewomon, *Riverfinger Women*, 16, 17.

115. Boyce Rensberger, "Letter to the Editor," *New York Times*, May 24, 2008.

116. William Bryk, "Dr. Feelgood," *New York Sun*, September 20, 2005.

117. Ibid.

118. Richard K. Weil, "Freedom at Windsor Mountain, Dewey's at Home Here," *Berkshire Eagle*, December 5, 1970.

119. Some of the offenses for which Heinz expelled students were unprecedented. For example, Cameron Melville '68–70, said he was kicked out for "hotwiring the school's bus in the middle of the night and taking a bunch of girls to Pittsfield for donuts." Melville, a major force in the creation of Helsinki Hudson, a successful club and restaurant in Hudson, New York, is also a musician under the name Bo Hammond. His family established the Melville Charitable Trust, and his grandfather was the creator of Thom McCann Shoes.

120. Jenny Anderson, "Retired Teacher at Mann Recalls Sex with Pupils," *New York Times*, June 24, 2012, 1, 4.

121. Marc Fisher, "The Master," *New Yorker*, April 1, 2013, 38–53.

122. W.E.B. Du Bois, *Darkwater* (New York: Washington Square Press, 2004).

123. *Time*, "Tivoli's Victorian Man," October 28, 1974.

124. Dennis McCarthy, "Player Piano Is a Time Machine," *Daily News*, July 31, 2008.

125. http://www.matuschka.net/bioPage.html; www.beautyoutofdamage.com.

126. Ralph E. Brown, "Hiss Urges Gov't Service Despite Watergate Incident," *Berkshire Eagle*, June 10, 1974.

Chapter 8

127. Doherty, *Tanglewood Campus*, 14. Doherty's inventory also contains references to the several parcels of land that Windsor Mountain School intermittently bought and sold while in Lenox.

128. "U.S. History, 1950–1975," www.elcoushistory.tripod.com/economics1970; Kim Phillips-Fein, "The Legacy of the 1970s Fiscal Crisis," www.thenation.com/legacy-1970's.html.

129. Doherty, *Tanglewood Campus*, 16.

130. Wexler, *Reared in a Greenhouse*, 230.

131. Susan Barlow, "Barlow School, Amenia, New York," www.archives. rootsweb.ancestry.com/barlow.

132. Amanda Korman, "Spirit of Service Remains Alive," *Berkshire Eagle*, October 16, 2011, B1, B5.

133. Bordentown Military Institute Alumni Association, www.bmicadets.org.

134. James F. Gill, *For James and Gillian: Jim Gill's New York* (New York: Fordham University Press, 2002).

135. Susan Besaw, "Foxhollow School Closing Because of Rising Costs," *Berkshire Eagle*, August 24, 1976, 1, 13; *New York Times*, "Aileen M. Farrell Dead at 83, Founder of Foxhollow School," December 21, 1981.

136. Berkshire Web, "Bellefontaine," http://www.berkshireweb.com/plexus/ cottages/bellefontaine/; Bellefontaine, "The History of Bellefontaine," http://www.bellefontaineihm.org/school/before_ihm.php.

137. David Wood, *Lenox*, 56.

138. Upper Housatonic Valley National Heritage Area, "The Guthrie Center at the Old Trinity Church, Great Barrington, Massachusetts," www.upperhousatonicheritage.org.

139. James Cass, "The School That Was."

140. Ibid.

141. *Berkshire Eagle*, "Holliston Jr. College Offers $350,000 for Windsor Mt. Site," November 5, 1975.

142. Doherty, *Tanglewood Campus*, 36, 40. In order to continue its base in the Berkshires, Bible Speaks West purchased the former Lenox School for Boys but was soon caught up in a scandal involving a local woman, Betsy Dovydenas, who, after leaving the church, sued Stevens for the money she gave him to buy the property. The lawsuit gained national attention, and she eventually was awarded the money, leading Bible Speaks to declare bankruptcy and to Stevens leaving the area in 1986. The property now belongs to Shakespeare and Company.

143. Mike Cunningham noted another use of the former Windsor/Winthrop property. In 1999–2000, Berkshire County Day School (1946–), a pre-K–9 private school in Stockbridge, decided to reinstate its high school and signed a ten-year lease from the Boston University Tanglewood Institute for the academic year only. The high school closed in 2007, but the school is still permitted to use the theater building.

Bibliography

African American Registry. "'A Better Chance' Founded." November 29, 2012.

Angress, Werner T. *Between Fear and Hope: Jewish Youth in the Third Reich*. Translated by Werner T. Angress and Christine Granger. New York: Columbia University Press, 1988.

Barnard, Hollinger F., ed. *Outside the Magic Circle: The Autobiography of Virginia Foster Durr*. Tuscaloosa: University of Alabama Press, 1990.

Bauer, Christian. *The Ritchie Boys*. DVD. 2007. http://www.ritchieboys.com.

Belafonte, Harry, with Michael Schnayerson. *My Song: A Memoir*. New York: Alfred A. Knopf, 2011.

Bondy, Max. "I Must Always Deal with It Until I Have Told You." In *Speeches to Young Germans (1926–1947)*. Dahlem, Germany: School Marienau Dahlem, 1998.

———. *Morning Talks*. Translated by Harald Baruschke and F.J. Gemmell. Surrey, UK: Thornton Heath, 1936.

———. "Talk Given by Dr. Max Bondy to German Young People After a Summer Spent in Europe—1947."

Cass, James. "The School That Was." Introduction to *A Fight For Human Rights: Hans Maeder's Politics of Optimism*, by Gunter Nabel. Frankfurt am Main, Germany: Dipa-Verlag, 1986.

Chartock, Roselle. *Educational Foundations*. Cranbury, NJ: Pearson Education, 2004.

———. "Talk on Bondy Philosophy at The Roeper School, October 26, 2011." http://vimeo.com/33663297.

Cohen, Herbert P., comp. "A Testament of the Survivors, a Memorial to the Dead: The Collection of Gross Breesen Letters and Related Materials." *Rundbriefe* (2002–05): 1–1540. http://grossbreesensilesia.com.

Cohodas, Nadine. *Queen: The Life and Music of Dinah Washington*. New York: Pantheon, 2004.

Collins, Judy. *Singing Lessons*. New York: Atria, 1999.

———. *Sweet Judy Blue Eyes: My Life in Music*. New York: Three Rivers Press, 2012.

Cramer, Ernst. "Curt Bondy and His Family." *Rundbriefe* (September 2002): 1393–94.

———. "In Memory of the Bondys." *Rundbriefe* (February 2005): 1447.

de Lone, Richard H., and Susan T. de Lone. "John Dewey Is Alive and Well in New England." In *The New World of Educational Thought*, edited by F.A. Stone. New York: MSS Information Corp., 1973.

Dictionary of American Family Names. New York: Oxford University Press, 2013.

Doherty, Jenn. *Boston University Tanglewood Campus*. Boston: Boston University Tanglewood Institute, 2012.

Dreier, Peter. *The 100 Greatest Americans of the 20th Century: A Social Justice Hall of Fame*. New York: Nation Books, 2012.

Eldridge, Maurice. Baccalaureate Address at the 2009 Swarthmore Commencement. http://www.swarthmore.edu/past-commencements/baccalaureate-address-maurice-eldridge-61.

Faas, Ekbert, with Maria Trombacco. *Robert Creeley: A Biography.* Lebanon, NH: University Press of New England, 2001.

Fisher, Marc. "The Master." *New Yorker*, April 1, 2013, 38–53.

Gialuco, John. "My Educational Experiences." *Camden Chronicles*, November 14, 2011.

Gillette, Robert H. *The Virginia Plan: William B. Thalhimer and a Rescue From Nazi Germany.* Charleston, SC: The History Press, 2011.

Gorres, Ida. *Broken Lights: Diaries and Letters of Ida Gorres, 1951–1959.* New York: Burns and Oates, 1964.

Jazz.com. "Rossi, Marc William." http://www.jazz.com/encyclopedia/rossi-marc-william.

Kane, Michele. "A Conversation with Annemarie Roeper: A View from the Self." *Roeper Review*, September 22, 2003, 1–5.

Kater, Michael H. *Different Drummers: Jazz in the Culture of Nazi Germany.* Oxford, UK: Oxford University Press, 2003.

Kelley, Robin D.G. *Thelonius Monk: The Life and Times of an American Original.* New York: Simon and Schuster, 2009.

Kersken, Barbara. *Report: Archive Marienau School.* Historical Research in Education, October 28, 2009. http://www.marienau.com/ueber-uns/das-sind-wir/archiv/.

Lamberti, Marjorie. "Radical School Teachers and the Origins of the Progressive Education Movement in Germany, 1900–1914." *History of Education Quarterly* 40 (Spring 2000): 22–48.

Laqueur, Walter. "The German Youth Movement and the 'Jewish Question': A Preliminary Survey." *Leo Baeck Institute Yearbook* VI (1961): 193–205.

———. *Young Germany: A History of the German Youth Movement.* New Brunswick, NJ: Transaction Inc., 1984.

Lloyd, Susan M. *The Putney School: A Progressive Experiment.* New Haven, CT: Yale University Press, 1987.

Mendes-Flohr, Paul R., and Jehuda Reinharz. *The Jew in the Modern World.* New York: Oxford University Press, 1995.

Nachman/Dykewomon, Elana. *Riverfinger Women.* Tallahassee, FL: Naiad Press Inc., 1992.

National Archives and Records. Franklin D. Roosevelt Presidential Library, Hyde Park, New York.

Neely, Richard. "What Was Windsor Like Just Before It Closed?" Posted in Windsor Mountain Online conversation, February 14, 2007.

Poitier-Henderson, Beverly. Authors Den. http://www.authorsden.com/visit/author.

Rockefeller, Steven C. *John Dewey: Religious Faith and Democratic Humanism.* New York: Columbia University Press, 1991.

Roeper, Annemarie, with Karen Mireau. *Marienau: A Daughter's Reflections.* Berkeley, CA: Azalea Art Press, 2012.

The Roeper School. "About Roeper." http://www.roeper.org/About-Roeper.

Ruff, Marcia. "An Education of Meaning: A Tribute to the Vision of George A. Roeper." In *A Centenary Celebration of George Alexander Roeper, September 7, 1910–August 24, 1992.* http://community.roeper.org/webadditions/RoeperCenPhotos.pdf.

Sachs, Ruth Hanna. "In Memoriam." *Roses at Noon: The Journal of the Center for White Rose Studies*, December 31, 2009. http://white-rose-studies.org/December_31_2009.html.

Shirley, Dennis. *The Politics of Progressive Education: The Odenwaldschule in Nazi Germany*. Cambridge, MA: Harvard University Press, 1992.

Veevers, Nick and Pete Allison. *Kurt Hahn: Inspirational, Visionary, Outdoor and Experiential Educator*. Rotterdam, Netherlands: Sense, 2011.

Weston, Randy. *African Rhythms: The Autobiography of Randy Weston*. Durham, NC: Duke University Press, 2010.

Wexler, Dorothy Bradford. *Reared in a Greenhouse: The Stories—and Story—of Dorothy Winthrop Bradford*. New York: Garland Publishing, 1998.

Wiener, Jan. *The Assassination of Heydrich: Hitler's Hangman and the Czech Resistance*. Bokeelia, FL: Irie Books, 2012.

Wood, David. *Lenox: Massachusetts Shire Town*. Lenox, MA: Published by the town of Lenox, 1969.

Yudkin, Jeremy. *The Lenox School of Jazz: A Vital Chapter in the History of American Music and Race Relations*. South Egremont, MA: Farshaw Publishing, 2006.

Interviews

Abramowicz, Mark (former student). Phone interview, October 3, 2011.
Albert, Lesley Larsen (alumni). Great Barrington, MA, October 18, 2012.
Belafonte, Adrienne (alumni). E-mail interview, January 18, 2013.
Belafonte, Shari (former student). E-mail interview, November 2, 2011.
Bellar, Dave (alumni). Great Barrington, MA, November 14, 2009.
Benford, Mac (faculty). Phone interview, March 14, 2014.
Blafield, Bob (faculty). Richmond, MA, January 14, 2013.
Bondy, Carolyn (faculty). E-mail interview, December 26, 2013.
Bondy, Eric (family). Phone interview, December 10, 2013.
Bondy, Heinz (headmaster). Germantown, Maryland, October 30, 2010.
Bondy, Peter (family). Phone interview, January 13, 2013.
Buchauer, Angela Longo (alumni). E-mail interview, January 16, 2013.
Buffington, Gigi (alumni). New York City, December 15, 2012.
Burstein, Fred (alumni). Great Barrington, MA, October 29, 2009.

Cohen-Hobbs, Barbara (alumni of Stockbridge School). West Stockbridge, MA, July 16, 2013.

Cunningham, Mike (current caretaker of former Windsor property). Lenox, MA, September 18, 2013.

Davis, Roger (alumni). Phone interview, September 9, 2013.

Dobbs, Bill (alumni). New York City, March 14, 2011.

Eldridge, Maurice (former assistant headmaster). New York City, April 10, 2014.

Esler, Pamela (alumni). Great Barrington, MA, May 16, 2013.

Fields, Linda (alumni). Phone interview, August 28, 2013.

Flynn, Terry (alumni of Cranwell). E-mail interview, February 25, 2010.

Getsinger, Ann (artist). Phone interview, September 16, 2013.

Greenfeld, Barbara Kronick (former student). Lenox, MA, December 2, 2011.

Gunn, Wray (son of faculty). Sheffield, MA, December 8, 2012.

Guthrie, Arlo (alumni of Stockbridge School). Email Interview, March 3, 2013.

Hall, Frances "Franny" Benn (faculty). Lenox, MA, November 3, 2009.

Hall, Terry (alumni). Lenox, MA, September 11, 2013.

Hasenclever, Wolf-Dieter (former headmaster at Schule Marienau). E-mail interview, February 8, 2011.

Hausman, Gerald (faculty). Phone interview, February 24, 2010.

Hemenway, Anne (alumni). Hudson, New York, October 1, 2010.

Hoolihan, Michael (faculty at Cornwall Academy). Great Barrington, MA, March 1, 2010.

Hoyt, Cathy (archivist in Vermont). E-mail interview, October 2, 2013.

Jackson, T.R. (former student). Phone interview, August 18, 2013.

Joseph, Stan (local historian). Phone interview, March 9, 2014.

Kegan, Daniel (alumni). Phone interview, September 3, 2013.

Kirsch, Daniel (alumni). E-mail interview, February 16, 2013.

Klein, Anne (faculty). Phone interview, April 10, 2011.

Kravette, Ellyn Reverend (alumni). E-mail interview, December 28, 2013.

Kusmin, Lorin (alumni). Phone interview, January 14, 2014.

Levin, Judy Kirsch (alumni). Lenox, MA, December 3, 2012.

Levis, Georgette Wasserstein (owner of Wilburton Inn). Manchester, VT, October 11, 2012.

Malcolm, Sarah (archivist at FDR Presidential Library). E-mail interview, February 16, 2011.

McCormick, Bob (alumni). Shutesbury, MA, October 2, 2013.

McWhorter, Jane (faculty). Phone interview, July 12, 2012.

Melville, Cameron (former student). Hudson, New York, May 20, 2011.

Mills, Benjamin (alumni). E-mail interview, January 22, 2014.

Mills, Cadman Atta (alumni). Phone interview, December 3, 2013.

Mireau, Karen (writer and publisher). Phone interview, October 13, 2013.

Motichka, Joanne (Matuschka) (alumni). New York City, March 10, 2014.

Neaman, Bob (alumni). Lenox, MA, July 13, 2010.

Parriott, Charlie (alumni). Phone interview, May 25, 2014.

Parriott, Susan (relative of alumni). Phone interview, October 23, 2013.

Peskin, Martha (wife of alumni). Lenox, MA, August 21, 2012.

Probandt, Alan (alumni). E-mail interview, January 3, 2014.

Putnam, Rob (former student). Great Barrington, MA, March 26, 2010.

Reinholt, Haldor and Genia (faculty). Lenox, MA, February 26, 2010.

Rhoad, Barbara (archivist in Vermont). E-mail interview, September 30, 2013.

Roeper, Annemarie Bondy (family). Phone interview, September 7, 2011.

Roeper, Peter (alumni and family). E-mail interview, June 21, 2013.

Roeper, Tom (family). Amherst, MA, August 16, 2011.

Roper, Jenny (family). New York City, December 9, 2011.

Ross, Stephan (Stephan Ross) (alumni). Needham, MA, December 28, 2009.

Ruff, Marcia (Roeper School historian). Bloomfield Hills, MI, October 16, 2012.

Shapiro, Jonathan (alumni). Phone interview, January 26, 2014.

Silberstein, Hadassah "Dossy" Pecker (alumni). Letter, March 28, 2014.

Smith, Christopher (alumni). Phone interview, March 4, 2014.

Steele, Nate (alumni). Phone interview, January 22, 2014.

Van Nostrand, Roselle (alumni). Great Barrington, MA, October 23, 2012.

Von Karolyi, Catya (former student). E-mail interview, May 16, 2013.

Weston, Caskey (alumni). Email interview, September 15, 2013.

Wexler, Eric (alumni). E-mail interview, December 28, 2013.

Whitehead, Jean Mercier (alumni). Great Barrington, MA, October 7, 2009.

Whitehead, Peter (alumni). Great Barrington, MA, September 19, 2013.

Whitney, Kathleen Gerard (family). E-mail interview, September 28, 2013.

Wiener, Zuzana (faculty and family). Lenox, MA, August 17, 2011.

Winner, Ellen (family). Phone interview, September 25, 2013.

Index

About the Author

R oselle Kline Chartock is professor emerita of education at the Massachusetts College of Liberal Arts in North Adams, Massachusetts, where she taught for twenty-five years. Her forty-five-year career also included teaching history at Monument Mountain Regional High School in Great Barrington, Massachusetts, for fifteen years and elementary and middle school for five years in Mamaroneck and Larchmont, New York. She is co-editor of the anthology *Can It Happen Again?: Chronicles of the Holocaust* (Black Dog and Leventhal, 1995), originally published as *The Holocaust Years: Society on Trial* (Bantam Books, Anti-Defamation League, 1978), and is author of *Educational Foundations: An Anthology* (Pearson, 2004) and *Strategies and Lessons for Culturally Responsive Teaching* (Pearson, 2010), as well as several articles in scholarly journals. Since 1971, Chartock has lived with her family in the Berkshire Hills, where she is now a writer and collage artist.

Courtesy of Marcia Ruff at The Roeper School.

www.ingramcontent.com/pod-product-compliance
Lightning Source LLC
Chambersburg PA
CBHW060800100426

42813CB00004B/886